Marx's Philosophy
of Revolution
and Freedom

Marx's Philosophy of Revolution and Freedom

A Critical Reconstruction

Mehmet Tabak

Marx's Philosophy of Revolution and Freedom: A Critical Reconstruction

Printed in the United States of America

ISBN: 978-1-939873-07-1 (Paperback)
ISBN: 979-8-604130-95-7 (Amazon)
ISBN: 978-1-939873-09-5 (Hardback)
ISBN: 978-1-939873-08-8 (E-book)

Library of Congress Control Number: 2020901135

Tabak, Mehmet.
Marx's Philosophy of Revolution and Freedom: A Critical Reconstruction
/ Mehmet Tabak
p. cm

Includes bibliographical references.

1. Karl Marx (1818-1883). 2. Philosophy—Ethics—Political Philosophy.
3. Human Nature—Alienation—Freedom. 3. Critique of Capitalism—
Revolution—Communism/Socialism. I. Title.

First Edition, 2020.

Contents

Preface and Acknowledgements

Nihil humani a me alienum puto.
(Nothing human is alien to me.)
—Marx's favorite maxim—

This book attempts to expound Marx's practical philosophy of freedom, to illustrate that a humanist ethics grounds it. It also provides important reasons to stress why he would have objected to an attempt of this kind. In other words, the philosophy of freedom this book attributes to him is purchased at the expense of his "historical-materialist" or "scientific" doctrine.

The first four chapters of this study explain the foundational terms of this philosophy. Accordingly, Chapter 1 examines his conception of human nature. *Inter alia*, it stresses how, and the sense in which, he identified human essence with freedom. Chapter 2 articulates his theory of human alienation in capitalism, which mostly hinges on the alienation of the worker. It maintains that he treated socio-economic alienation essentially as unfreedom, and so as dehumanization in this sense. Chapter 3 illustrates how the theory of alienation also informs his conception of the modern-capitalist state. By extension, this means that he regarded the state as inherently antithetical to freedom—to be abolished in communism. Chapter 4 validates the claim that he condemned capitalism's alienation-unfreedom nexus on humanist-ethical grounds.[1]

The subsequent three chapters examine Marx's approach to revolution from various vantage points. Chapter 5 retrieves his humanist-ethical justification of revolution as a necessary process to abolish alienation.[2] Chapter 6 documents the practical grounds of his revolutionary gradualism and its link to the strategy to urge the proletariat to win the struggle for democracy.[3] As Chapter 7 illustrates, Marx was against any top-down version of revolution and constructing socialism. Instead, he consistently defended the principle and strategy of the proletariat's self-emancipation.[4]

---

[1] Chapter 4 also illustrates Marx's disparagement of all ethical assessments.
[2] Chapter 5 also documents Marx's historical-materialist or "scientific" declaration of revolution as inevitable.
[3] Chapter 6 also accounts for Marx's brief putschist years.
[4] Chapter 7 also notes Marx's statism during his "Blanquist" years.

Practically speaking, this strategy calls for the development of the "sprouts" of the future society, such as the workers' co-operatives and political associations, within capitalism. Philosophically speaking, it envisions a process of self-dealienation. Thus, the chapter defines Marx's idea of revolution essentially as a gradual process of self-emancipation from the conditions of alienation.

Chapter 8 articulates Marx's image of socialism or communism,[5] the classless society or utopia to be constructed in the future.[6] It deals with a host of related issues, such as the dictatorship of the proletariat, the principles of distribution, and free activity. It highlights the fact that his image of communism is ultimately built upon his humanist philosophy of freedom. As such, communism is conceived as the positive transcendence of alienation, and so as the realm of freedom. Marx's utopia thus reflects what he took to be the general conditions "most favorable to, and worthy of ..., human nature" (Marx).

It seems obligatory nowadays to explain the relevance of a great thinker's ideas *for us today*. This is especially true of the studies on Marx's ideas. The present study unburdens Marx, as well as its author, of this obligation. It also does not discuss the issue of how, or whether, his followers later distorted his thoughts and/or misapplied them. There are many other things this study does not attempt to do. Suffice it to say, and to repeat, it is strictly an attempt to critically reconstruct Marx's practical philosophy of freedom. This self-limiting approach is urged by my desire to focus on the task at hand, to keep it manageable both for myself and the reader. It is hoped that the reader will find it informative and interesting, and perhaps even relevant and useful *for us today*.

Suna Buse Agkoc, Jaella Brockmann, Kyoungseo (Emma) Hong, Dena Motevalian, Tyson Patros, Shinasi Rama, and Akiko Tabak have provided useful feedback on an earlier draft of this study. I sincerely thank them all.

---

[5] Marx used these two terms, as well as "association of free producers," interchangeably. For an informed discussion, see Chattopadhyay, *Socialism and Commodity Production*, Ch. 1.

[6] Chapter 8 first illustrates, and then brackets out, Marx's wholesale disparagement of utopianism, as well as his denial of having ever himself engaged in utopian thinking—or envisioning a future society.

Human Nature

1.1 Introduction

Many legends about Marx's thought still abound. One of them finds its most famous expression in Louis Althusser's claim that the related concepts of human essence or nature[1] and alienation, propounded by the young Marx, "exploded" in his subsequent works. "The result of this explosion was the evaporation of the notions of subject, human essence, and alienation, which disappear completely ... in *Capital*.[2] This chapter debunks this legend indirectly; it reconstructs Marx's concept of human nature with material drawn from his early and later works, including *Capital*.[3] Chapter 2 likewise illustrates his continued utilization of the concept of alienation.

Marx's conception of human nature is crucial to understanding his practical philosophy of freedom. The sense in which it is so will be demonstrated in the subsequent chapters. The present chapter simply outlines the most basic aspects of his conception of it. To this end, 1.2 first discusses his criticism of several prevailing notions of human nature, especially the ones that regard the alienated or "isolated" individual in bourgeois society as the universal individual. It then illustrates that Marx himself conceived the individual as essentially a social being. The subsequent section discusses Marx's understanding of human nature through the concept of needs, arguing that his emphasis in this regard was on how the objects of needs are produced, that is, on what he regarded as uniquely *human* activity (1.3). This focus also informs the main

---

[1] I use human *nature* and *essence* interchangeably throughout this study. They both refer to a set of permanent human characteristics, a subset of which is uniquely *human*.

[2] Althusser, *Lenin and Philosophy and Other Essays*, 120–121. Many others have repeated similar versions of this legend. Perhaps the most surprising in this regard is István Mészáros, *Marx's Theory of Alienation*, 13–14.

[3] For a compelling explication of the humanist grounds of *Capital*, see Dunayevskaya, *Marxism and Freedom*, 103-25. As she puts it elsewhere, "Humanism gives Marx's magnum opus its force and direction." Dunayevskaya, "Marx's Humanism Today," 63.

theme of 1.4, which considers Marx's understanding of human nature via the concept of free objective activity, through which individuals engage in not only production but also self-realization and development (1.4).

1.2 *Zoon Politikon*

The underlying principle of Marx's critique of other theories of human nature can be found in his "Theses on Feuerbach." As the ninth thesis states, "The highest point reached by contemplative materialism," including that of Ludwig Feuerbach, "is the contemplation of single individuals and of civil society."[4] Marx further elaborates upon this conceptual problem in *Grundrisse*:

> The individual and isolated hunter and fisherman, who serves Adam Smith and Ricardo as a starting point, is one of the unimaginative fantasies of the 18th century … No more is Rousseau's *contrat social*, which by means of a social contract establishes a relationship and connection between subjects that are by nature independent [isolated], based on this kind of naturalism. This is … the anticipation of "bourgeois society," which began to evolve in the 16th century and was making giant strides toward maturity in the 18th … The prophets of the 18th century, on whose shoulders Smith and Ricardo were still standing completely, envisaged this 18th-century individual … as an ideal whose existence belonged to the past. They saw this individual not as an historical result, but as the starting point of history; not as something evolving in the course of history, but posited by nature, because for them this individual was the natural individual, according to their idea of human nature.[5]

Thus, "*bourgeois* relations are … quietly substituted as irrefutable natural laws of society in *abstracto*." Put another way, "Man becomes [or has become] individualized only through the process of history. Originally, he is a *species being*."[6]

---

[4] Marx, "Theses on Feuerbach," 3–5.
[5] Marx, *Outlines of the Critique of Political Economy* (*Grundrisse*), *MECW* 28: 17-18. All citations of those works that appear in multiple volumes of *Marx and Engels Collected Works* include the acronym *MECW*, followed by the relevant volume number.
[6] Ibid., 25, 420.

Marx's claim that this "isolated" individual is a historical product does not necessarily imply a wholesale rejection of all conceptions of universal, transhistorical, or permanent human nature. As Norman Geras aptly points out, "It is an elementary logical point ... that to declare of anything that it changes does not commit one to the view that *everything* about it changes or that it has *no* enduring features."[7]

Indeed, Marx's claim that "Originally, he is a *species being*" is not simply a historical claim about the social nature of our ancestors. It is also a statement about human essence in general. We know this because his above critique of the "bourgeois" notions of human nature is preceded by a formulation of his own conception of universal human nature: "Man is a [*zoon politikon*] in the most literal [not *political*] sense: he is not only a social animal, but an animal that can isolate itself only within a society."[8] As he further clarifies in the *Manuscripts of 1844*, this means that "In creating a world of objects by his practical activity, in his work upon inorganic nature, man proves himself a conscious species-being, i.e., as a being that [knowingly] treats the species as its own essential being, or that treats itself as a species-being."[9]

Overall,

> The individual *is the social being.* His manifestations of life— even if they may not appear in the direct form of *communal* manifestations of life carried out in association with others [which is the case in bourgeois society]—are therefore an expression and confirmation of *social life.* Man's individual and species-life are not *different,* however much—and this is inevitable—the mode of existence of the individual is a more *particular* or more *general* mode of the life of the species.[10]

---

[7] Geras, *Marx and Human Nature*, 90. For other useful articulations of Marx's conception of human nature, see Fromm, *Marx's Concept of Man*; Schaff, *Marxism and the Human Individual*; Ollman, *Alienation*, 73–126; Elster, *Making Sense of Marx*, 61–82; Wood, *Karl Marx,* 16–43; Tabak, *Dialectics of Human Nature in Marx's Philosophy*, 1-24

[8] Marx, *Outlines of the Critique of Political Economy (Grundrisse)*, *MECW* 28: 18.

[9] Marx, *Economic and Philosophic Manuscripts of 1844*, 276.

[10] Ibid., 298-99.

To recapitulate, human beings have always been social, even in the very (bourgeois) society in which their isolation from each other appears to be the ideological and practical norm. Thus, the egotistical individual of bourgeois society is both alienated from his or her species-essence and remains, in potentiality, unalienated (see Chapter 2). Indeed, according to this view, one cannot experience alienation, or escape from it, unless one is simultaneously unalienated in potentiality.

1.3 Needs and Production

The concept of needs also serves as a humanist yardstick with which Marx differentiates socialism from capitalism—or promotes the former and disparages the latter.[11] This double-sided import of the concept will be explored in the ensuing chapters. The aim of this brief section is to provide a general sense of how he conceived needs and to point out that his conception of them is "fundamental in Marx's theory of human nature."[12]

Although their importance to his overall oeuvre is undeniable, Marx did not provide a systematic analysis of needs. His articulation of them requires piecing together what are otherwise dispersed commentaries, found in his various works. Luckily, Agnes Heller has already done this in a remarkable manner.[13] The taxonomy of needs that emerges from her analysis resembles Abraham H. Maslow's "the hierarch of needs," extending from the basic-natural needs to the need for self-actualization.[14]

Moreover, Marx's approach to needs has the same structure as his conception of human nature, meaning that human needs, too, are shown to be both permanent and historically and socially modified, as are human powers and the manner of asserting them:

---

[11] "We have seen what significance, given socialism, the *wealth* of human needs acquires, and what significance, therefore, both a *new mode of production* and a new *object* of production obtain: a new manifestation of the forces of human nature and a new enrichment of *human* nature. Under private property [capitalism] their significance is reversed." Marx, *Economic and Philosophic Manuscripts of 1844*, 306.

[12] Elster, *Making Sense of Marx*, 68.

[13] Heller, *The Theory of Need in Marx*. Also see Mandel, *Power and Money*, 205-14; Chitty, "The Early Marx on Needs," 23-31.

[14] Maslow, *Motivation and Personality*.

His natural wants, such as food, clothing, fuel and housing, vary according to the climatic and other physical conditions of his country. On the other hand, the number and extent of his so-called necessary wants, as also the modes of satisfying them, are themselves the product of historical development, and depend therefore to a great extent on the degree of civilization of a country, more particularly on the conditions under which, and consequently on the habits and degree of comfort.[15]

In "Wage Labor and Capital," Marx also acknowledges the subjective-psychological determination of needs:

A house may be large or small; as long as the neighboring houses are likewise small, it satisfies all social demands for a dwelling. But let a palace arise beside the little house, and it shrinks from a little house to a hut. The little house shows now that its owner has only very slight or no demands to make; and however high it may shoot up in the course of civilization, if the neighboring palace grows to an equal or even greater extent, the occupant of the relatively small house will feel more and more uncomfortable, dissatisfied, and cramped within its four walls.[16]

Nevertheless, he does not here intend to propose a psychology of needs per se. Rather, his aim is to argue that they are socially and relationally determined in an important sense. For instance, given the unequal distribution of wealth in capitalism, the needs of workers are of necessity inadequately satisfied, *even if* their income increases:

An appreciable rise in wages presupposes a rapid growth of productive capital. Rapid growth of productive capital calls forth just as rapid a growth of wealth, of luxury, of social needs and social pleasures. Therefore, although the pleasures of the

---

[15] Marx, *Capital*, Vol. 1, 181. "Hunger is hunger, but hunger that is satisfied by cooked meat eaten with knife and fork differs from hunger that devours raw meat with the help of hands, nails, and teeth. Production thus produces not only the object but also the manner of consumption, not only objectively but also subjectively." Marx, *Outlines of the Critique of Political Economy, MECW* 28: 29.

[16] Marx, "Wage Labor and Capital," 216.

laborer have increased, the social gratification which they afford has fallen in comparison with the increased pleasures of the capitalist, which are inaccessible to the worker, in comparison with the stage of development of society in general. Our wants and pleasures have their origin in society; we therefore measure them in relation to society; we do not measure them in relation to the objects which serve for their gratification. Since they are of a social nature, they are of a relative nature.[17]

This passage should not be read as a defense of the absurd view that all needs are strictly socially determined. To use the example from the previous passage, his argument is not that the need for a dwelling has its origin in society. Rather, it is that the measure of a dwelling one needs in a specific society, both qualitatively and quantitatively speaking, is socially conditioned. Be this as it may, in order to grasp the most crucial link Marx seeks to establish between needs and human nature, it is necessary to bracket out the historical and social determination of needs.

A systematic reconsideration of Marx's comments on needs would show that his focus is primarily on the activity to appropriate from the external nature, or else to produce by interacting with it, the objects of their satisfaction. And, herein lies the crucial link he seeks to establish between needs and human nature. In other words, the mode of interacting with the external nature reveals what it means to be distinctively human. Marx refers to this process as "objective activity," "life activity," or "production."

The first thing to consider in this regard is why there is objective activity in the first place. Following Feuerbach,[18] Marx points out that "Neither nature objectively nor nature subjectively is directly given in a form adequate to the *human* being." In other words, humans are born with needs, which can be satisfied with objects "outside" them. These are "essential *objects*, indispensable to the manifestation and confirmation of his powers." For example, "*Hunger* is a natural *need*; it therefore needs a *nature* [i.e. objects of consumption] outside itself, in order to satisfy itself, to be stilled"[19]

---

[17] Ibid.

[18] See Feuerbach, "Preliminary Theses on the Reform of Philosophy," 51.

[19] Marx, *Economic and Philosophic Manuscripts of 1844*, 336–37.

In *The German Ideology*, Marx (together with Engels) makes this activity the basis of his philosophy of history.

> The first premise of all human existence, and, therefore, of all history . . . (is that) men must be in a position to live in order to be able to "make history." But life involves before everything else eating and drinking, housing, clothing and various other things. The first historical act is thus the production of the means to satisfy these needs, the production of the material life itself.[20]

"The second point [or premise] is that the satisfaction of the first need, the action of satisfying, and the instruments of satisfaction which have been acquired, lead to new needs." The way these acts occur is uniquely human, as we will observe later in this chapter. What needs to be stressed here is that, in an important sense, history for Marx embodies changing needs and the changing manner or mode in which they are satisfied. "The third circumstance which, from the very outset, enters into historical development, is that men, who daily remake their own life, begin to make other men, to propagate their kind: the relation between man and woman, parents and children, the *family*." As Marx crucially clarifies, "These three aspects of social activity are not of course to be taken as three different stages, but just as three aspects or ... three 'moments', which have existed simultaneously since the dawn of history ... and which still assert themselves in history today."[21]

Otherwise put, Marx here articulates the transhistorical *modus operandi* and *vivendi* of humankind, arguing that, by their nature, human beings are social and that they actively and collectively create/produce the objects of their needs as well as the means by which they produce these objects. Also, producing to satisfy the needs of other individuals is a unique and higher *human* attribute, and this "shows that as a *human being* each transcends his own particular needs."[22]

---

[20] Marx and Engels, *The German Ideology*, 42–43; also see 31.
[21] Ibid., 43.
[22] Marx, *Outlines of the Critique of Political Economy* (*Grundrisse*), *MECW* 28: 174-75. All citations of those works that appear in multiple

1.4 Free Activity and Human Flourishing

As anticipated already, Marx thinks objective activity (labor) itself is a need.[23] It "is a necessary condition, independent of all forms of society, for the existence of the human race," he writes in the first volume of *Capital,* adding that "it is an eternal nature-imposed necessity, without which there can be no material exchanges between man and Nature, and therefore [no need satisfaction and so] no life."[24] A similar thought occurs in the third volume of *Capital*: "Man" must "wrestle with Nature to satisfy his wants, to maintain and reproduce life ... and he must do this in all social formations and under all possible social formations."[25] Ultimately, then, Marx's economic theory, like his philosophy of history, is human-centric: "Man himself is the basis of his material production, as of any other production that he carries on."[26]

An important issue to consider in this section is the kind of work or activity Marx regarded as uniquely human. In his various works, he repeatedly resorts to the old-school method deriving *human* characteristics from comparisons to other animals.[27] An example of this is found in *Capital*: "The use and fabrication of instruments of labor, although existing in the germ among certain species of animals, is specifically characteristic of the human labor process, and Franklin therefore defines man as a tool-making animal."[28] This is one reason why human beings are able to develop their organic and inorganic capacities, and behind this lurks the human capacity to act consciously and learn.

Marx uses the same method in the *Manuscripts of 1844* to reveal notable differences between human and animal activity. One of

---

volumes of *Marx and Engels Collected Works* include the acronym *MECW,* followed by the relevant volume number.

[23] Heller, *The Theory of Need in Marx,* 42.

[24] Marx, *Capital,* Vol.1, 53. For a very valuable reconstruction of Marx's philosophical concept of nature, see Schmidt, *The Concept of Nature in Marx.*

[25] Marx, *Capital,* Vol 3, 807.

[26] Marx, *Economic Manuscript of 1861-63, MECW* 31: 185

[27] For an interesting and informed discussion of this issue, see Wallimann, *Estrangement: Marx's Conception of Human Nature and the Division of Labor,* Ch. 2.

[28] Marx, *Capital,* Vol. 1, 189.

them is that the animal "produces only under the dominion of immediate physical need, whilst man produces even when he is free from physical need and *only truly produces in freedom therefrom* [emphasis added]." Here, he formulates the famous distinction between free activity within the sphere of necessity and beyond this sphere, and clearly ranks the latter higher (also see 8.5), due to its consistency with the dictates of human essence.

Moreover,

> The animal is immediately one with its life-activity. It does not distinguish itself from it. It is *its life-activity*. Man makes his life-activity itself the object of his will and of his consciousness. He has conscious life-activity. It is not a determination with which he directly merges. Conscious life-activity distinguishes man immediately from animal life-activity ... Only because of that is his activity free activity.[29]

Another version of this thought appears in *Capital*:

> We presuppose labor in a form that stamps it as exclusively human. A [spider's] operations ... resemble those of a weaver, and a bee puts to shame many an architect in the construction of her cells. But what distinguishes the worst architect from the best of bees is this, that the architect raises his structure in imagination before he erects it in reality. At the end of every labor-process, we get a result that already existed in the imagination [consciousness] of the laborer at its commencement. He not only effects a change of form in the material on which he works, but also realizes a purpose of his own that gives the law to his *modus operandi*, and to which [purpose] he must subordinate his will. [30]

According to Marx, then, free activity is itself a need—indeed the highest of human needs—not least because it is the defining aspect of human essence.[31] Its satisfaction depends on the coincidence of the individual's self-given *purpose* and *activity*.

---

[29] Marx, *Economic and Philosophic Manuscripts of 1844*, 276.

[30] Marx, *Capital*, Vol. 1, 187–88.

[31] "Freedom of the will," writes the young Marx accordingly, "is inherent in human nature"; freedom is "the essence of man." Marx, "Debates on Freedom of the Press," 137, 155.

Reversely put, externally determined activity appears to be "forced" upon the subject since it is contrary to his or her essence. Accordingly, "the less he is attracted by the nature of the work and the mode in which it is carried on," he argues in *Capital*, "the less ... he enjoys it as something which gives play to his bodily and mental powers."[32] As we will see in the next chapter, Marx regards this as a fundamental form of alienation, on which capitalist production significantly hinges.

In Marx's view, free activity is not only a higher need but also the kind of activity needed to convert productive activity into a process of self-realization and development (flourishing). In this sort of activity, "[man] develops his own slumbering powers and compels them to act in obedience to his sway."[33] Differently put, in truly free activity, "the external aims are stripped of their character as merely external natural necessity, and become posited as aims which only the individual himself posits, that they are therefore posited as self-realization, objectification of the subject, and thus real freedom, whose action is, precisely work."[34]

In short, Marx regarded the *capacity* for self-development as an inherent human-species characteristic. As such, it is an essential need. This thought informs his dynamic explanation of the changes that occur in the sphere of needs and powers. As he maintains in the *Grundrisse*, "in the act of reproduction ..., the producers ... transform themselves in that they ... [develop] new qualities from within themselves, develop through production new powers and new ideas, new modes of intercourse, new needs, and new speech."[35] "For this reason," and elsewhere, human reality "is just as highly varied as the *determinations* of human *essence* and *activities*."[36]

---

[32] Marx, *Capital*, Vol. 1, 188.

[33] Ibid.

[34] Marx, *Outlines of the Critique of Political Economy*, MECW 28: 530.

[35] Marx, *Outlines of the Critique of Political Economy*, MECW 28, 418. "Originally, human needs [are] ... slight. They themselves grow with the development of the productive forces" (ibid., 531).

[36] Marx, *Economic and Philosophic Manuscripts of 1844*, 299-300.

***

In *Capital*, Marx issues the following polemic against Jeremy Bentham:

> To know what is useful for a dog, one must study dog-nature. This nature is not to be deduced from the principle of utility. Applying this to man, he that would evaluate [*beurteilen*] all human acts, movements, relations, etc., by the principle of utility, must first deal with human nature in general, and then with human nature as historically modified in each epoch. Bentham makes short work of it. With the driest naiveté he takes the modern petit-bourgeois man [*Spießbürger*], especially the English one, as the normal man. Whatever is useful to this strange normal man, and to his world, is absolutely useful.[37]

This passage proves Marx's commitment to the concept of human nature in a "mature" work. It also justifies my claim that he conceived human nature simultaneously in its "general" and "historically modified" forms. More significant for the purposes of this study is the humanist "principle of utility" he suggests in this passage against Bentham's principle. This is to say, as the present study intends to illustrate, Marx's practical philosophy of emancipation-freedom hinges on his conception of human nature, which, *inter alia*, is utilized to determine what is good and harmful to human beings in a limited, but fundamental nevertheless, sphere of life, namely, the system production. The first step to be taken in this regard is to articulate the practical *negation* of human nature, which Marx presents as alienation in capitalism.

---

[37] Marx, *Capital,* Vol. 1, 605 n. 2. Translation slightly modified.

Alienation

2.1 Introduction

If it is not already, it should become obvious shortly that the theory of alienation presupposes the theory of human nature. As a relation of the concept of human nature, the term "alienation" refers to "dehumanization." It will be seen that the whole thing hinges on the concept of unfreedom, just as the general theory of human nature hinges on freedom.

The present chapter outlines Marx's theory of human alienation or estrangement[1] in capitalist society,[2] especially as it is revealed in the experience of the worker. As Ollman aptly puts it, "Marx presents alienation as a partaking of four broad relations which [are] ... man's relations to his productive activity, his product, other men and the species."[3] Following Ollman's useful schema, this chapter reconstructs Marx's theory of alienation by beginning with his analysis of alienated activity (2.2), followed by alienation from the products of labor (2.3), other individuals (2.4), and the human species (2.5). However, the attentive reader will have noticed that the list could be longer or categorized somewhat differently.[4]

2.2 Alienated Activity

According to Marx, the alienated character of the worker's productive activity, the activity of need-satisfaction, consists in the fact that it "is not his own, but someone else's, that it does not belong

---

[1] "Alienation" (*Entäusserung*) and "estrangement" *(Entfremdung)* are used interchangeably.

[2] His rather scarce comments on this issue indicate that Marx thought various forms of alienation existed in non-capitalist societies. See Wallimann, *Estrangement*, Ch. 8.

[3] Ollman, *Alienation*, 136. In addition to Ollman's seminal work, this chapter is indebted to, among others, Fromm, *Marx's Concept of Man*; Mészáros, *Marx's Theory of Alienation*; Wallimann, *Estrangement*; Sayers, *Marx and Alienation*.

[4] As we will see in due course, especially in Chapter 7, Marx does not regard workers as completely alienated, even though some of his comments appear to suggest otherwise. Here, we assume he does for strictly analytical purposes.

to him, that in it he belongs, not to himself, but to another." This constitutes alienation in two different senses. First, the worker transfers (alienates) his/her productive powers to the capitalist, who commands his/her activity. In this scenario, the worker's activity is not a purposive, self-posited, free activity. "His labor is therefore not voluntary." Herein lies the second sense of alienated activity. As Marx puts it, this form of "labor is external to the worker, i.e., it does not belong to his intrinsic nature." Consequently, the worker, as a *human* being, "does not affirm himself but denies himself, does not feel content but unhappy, does not develop freely his physical and mental energy but mortifies his body and ruins his mind." Marx goes so far as to argue that "external labor, labor in which man alienates himself, is a labor of self-sacrifice, of mortification."[5]

The "mature" Marx repeats similar thoughts, describing alienated labor as "the exertion of the worker as a natural force drilled in a particular way." Such "work is always repulsive and always appears as *externally imposed, forced labor.*" This "*activity* is ... *hateful* ..., a *torment,* and rather the *semblance* of an activity." It is the antithesis of "*travail attractif,*" which must be consistent with "the self-realization of the individual."[6]

In his various works, Marx also consistently disparages the way this "*semblance* of an activity" comes into being, or rather is repeatedly reproduced, in capitalism. In order to get to the bottom of this problem, he distinguishes between labor power and labor (activity), especially in his later works. It is the former that the dispossessed worker is compelled to sell to the capitalist.[7] Consequently, the labor power of the worker becomes a commodity. As Marx sees it, this entails the commodification of *human* powers, and so of persons since labor power is "the aggregate of those mental and physical capabilities existing in the physical form, the living personality, of a human being."[8]

[5] Marx, *Economic and Philosophic Manuscripts of 1844*, 274.
[6] Marx, *Outlines of the Critique of Political Economy*, MECW 28: 530. All citations of those works that appear in multiple volumes of *Marx and Engels Collected Works* include the acronym *MECW*, followed by the relevant volume number.
[7] For a competent analysis of "dispossession" in Marx's analysis, see Harvey, *A Companion to Marx's* Capital, Ch. 11.
[8] Marx, *Capital*, Vol. 1, 177.

Labor, on the other hand, is the exercise, the externalization, the "expenditure" of these human powers or capabilities. The capitalist purchases the former, and so acquires the right to control the activity of workers, who consequently become "the slaves of capital."[9] By the way, Marx's take on this issue implies that workers are *collectively* the "slaves" of the capitalist class, unlike the traditional chattel slavery.

The main purpose of buying the labor power of an individual in capitalism is to convert him or her into a special power of production, which not only produces commodities but also continuously reproduces itself as a value-adding commodity. This process degrades human beings into *things*. In all this, "the bourgeois sees in the proletarian not a *human being,* but a *force* capable of creating wealth, a force which can then compare with other productive forces—an animal, a machine."[10] This process constitutes a form of mutual dehumanization since the dehumanizer himself/herself is also alienated in the process—on account of treating fellow human beings merely as means.

As the young Marx puts it,

> Production (in capitalism) does not simply produce man as a *commodity*, the *human commodity,* man in the role of *commodity*; it produces him in keeping with this role as a *mentally* and physically dehumanized being.—Immorality, deformity, and dulling of the workers and the capitalists.—Its product is *the self-conscious and self-acting commodity* ... the *human* commodity.[11]

Put from another angle, and with a dose of sarcasm, the wage-laborer is "free in the double sense, that as a free man he can dispose of his labor power as his own commodity, and that on the other hand he has no other commodity for sale, is short of everything necessary for the realization of his labor power."[12] For this reason, too, Marx thinks this so-called "free" labor is indeed forced labor.

---

[9] Ibid. Also see Marx, *Outlines of the Critique of Political Economy*, *MECW* 28: 530.

[10] Marx, "Draft of an Article on Friedrich List's Book *Das nationale System der politischen Oekonomie*," 286.

[11] Marx, *Economic and Philosophic Manuscripts of 1844*, 284.

[12] Marx, *Capital*, Vol. 1, 179.

This scenario is constantly reproduced in capitalism:

It is no longer a mere accident that capitalist and laborer confront each other in the market as buyer and seller. It is the process itself that incessantly hurls back the laborer onto the market as a vendor of his labor power, and that incessantly converts his own product into a means by which another man can purchase him. In reality, the laborer belongs to capital before he has sold himself to capital. His economic bondage is both brought about and concealed by the periodic sale of himself, by his change of masters, and by the oscillations in the market price of labor power.[13]

The "economic bondage" resulting from this continuous commodification of labor power produces, and reproduces, as *Capital* again states, the "undisputed authority of the capitalist over men, (who) are but parts of a mechanism that belongs to him."[14] This bondage constitutes a structural relation of authority, social and political (see Chapter 3), as well as a relation of alienated property.

2.3 Alienation from the Products of Labor
In *The German Ideology*, Marx and Engels posit a rhetorical question: "How does it happen that their relations [and products] assume an independent existence over against ... [individuals], and that the forces of their own life become superior to them?"[15] As we will see shortly, Marx calls this situation "fetishism," which is the crux of the form of alienation now under our scrutiny.

At bottom, the second form of alienation, which Marx also calls "the alienation of the worker *in* his product [emphasis added]," is very simple: The worker is hired to produce commodities for the capitalist, who intends to recapture their value by selling them to others. Thus, the product is alienated to the capitalist; it becomes *his/her* private property, not the property of the direct producer. However, this aspect of alienation also entails the fact that "the

---

[13] Ibid., 577. "The slave is sold once and for all; the proletarian has to sell himself by the day and by the hour." Engels, "Principles of Communism," 343-44.
[14] Marx, *Capital*, Vol. 1, 361.
[15] Marx and Engels, *The German Ideology*, 93.

worker is related to *the product of his labor* as to an *alien object*," meaning that the worker's product appear to "exists *outside him, independently*, as something alien to him," as "a power on its own confronting him ... as something hostile and alien."[16] These thoughts need to be unpacked.

As Marx points out, "a thing can be useful, and the product of human labor, without being a commodity. Whoever directly satisfies his wants [or needs] with the produce of his own labor creates, indeed, use values, but not commodities," which are defined primarily in terms of their exchange value. "To become a commodity a product must be transferred to another, whom it will serve as a use value, by means of an exchange."[17] For good or ill, Marx here reserves the definition of commodity strictly for the products produced by wage-labor, which are alienated to the capitalist, who sells them to others.

Thus, the worker is alienated from the product in a simple sense, in that what he or she produces belongs to the capitalist. At the same time, the same act counts as alienation in a related but different sense, viz., the *purpose* of the product, and of producing it, is alien to its natural purpose, which is the direct satisfaction of human (individual or social) needs. Otherwise said, from the perspective of the individual capitalist, the purpose of production is profit, though, from a systemic point of view, it is ultimately the accumulation of capital.[18] Consequently, the satisfaction of the needs of individuals, especially of workers, takes on a subordinate status in capitalism.

Also, the worker exists for the sake of producing wealth. Indeed, this is also true of the capitalist, *mutatis mutandis*. As Marx explains in the *Grundrisse*, in capitalism, "enrichment is an end in itself. The activity corresponding to the purpose of capital can only be that of enrichment, i.e. that of its own increase and multiplication."[19] This is not merely an "economic" observation. In "the modern [capitalistic] world," he argues in the same text, "production appears as the aim of mankind and wealth as the aim of production." This "narrow bourgeois form," this alienated practice, appears irrational and condemnable form a humanistic point of view:

[16] Marx, *Economic and Philosophic Manuscripts of 1844*, 272.

[17] Marx, *Capital*, Vol. 1, 50–51.

[18] Ibid., 51.

[19] Marx, *Outlines of the Critique of Political Economy*, MECW 28, 200.

In the bourgeois economy [the science]—and in the epoch of production to which it corresponds—this complete unfolding of man's inner potentiality turns into his total emptying-out. His universal objectification becomes his total alienation, and the demolition of all determined one-sided aims becomes the sacrifice of the [human] end-in-itself to a wholly external purpose.[20]

"It cannot be otherwise," Marx insists in *Capital*, "in a mode of production in which the laborer exists to satisfy the needs of self-expansion of existing values, instead of, on the contrary, material wealth existing to satisfy the needs of development on the part of the laborer."[21] Here, alienation presents itself as a double-relation. On the one hand, the products of labor acquire a different purpose than the natural-human one. On the other, and relatedly, the laborer's life turns into an appendage of capital, of the accumulation of wealth. Analogously put, capital is a "vampire-like ... dead labor," which "only lives by sucking living labor, and lives the more, the more labor it sucks."[22]

More mundanely put, in capitalism, it is

no longer the laborer that employs the means of production, but the means of production that employ the laborer. Instead of being consumed by him as material elements of his productive activity, they consume him as the ferment necessary to their own life-process, and the life-process of capital consists only in its movement as value constantly expanding, constantly multiplying itself.[23]

Marx calls the form of alienation implied in this passage "fetishism." "Fetishism," writes he, refers to any condition in which "the productions of the human brain ... and the products of men's hands ... *appear* as independent beings ..., entering into relation both with one another and the human race [emphasis added]."[24] In

---

[20] Ibid., 411-12.
[21] Marx, *Capital*, Vol. 1, 616.
[22] Ibid., 241.
[23] Ibid., 314-15.
[24] Ibid., 83.

all instances of fetishism, their own products (mental and material) come to dominate human beings in some sense. Religion, god, the state, and even the capitalists are but various forms of such fetishistic "independent beings," according to Marx. So is capital. Therefore,

> all the productive powers as the general social form ... present themselves as productive powers and forms of capital, of *objectified* labor, of the objective conditions of labor, which— as such an independent entity—are personified in the capitalist and confront living labor. Here once again we have the inversion of the relation, the expression of which we have already characterized as *fetishism*.[25]

In this context, Marx draws our attention to a "paradox," unimaginable, he reckons, even to the great thinkers of the past. The paradox is this: Instead of giving the worker more security in maintaining his/her life, capital, as immensely productive power, "dispels all fixity and security in the situation of the laborer" by making him/her "superfluous," thus giving way to the "creation of that monstrosity, an industrial reserve army, kept in misery in order to be always at the disposal of capital." This further leads to "the most reckless squandering of labor power," to the exploitation of ever cheapening labor power.[26]

Moreover, according to Marx, the instruments of production, such as machinery, *literally* turn into instruments of control, helping place workers "under the command of a perfect hierarchy of officers and sergeants." Under such a system of command, he and Engels observe in the *Manifesto*, not only are workers "slaves of the bourgeois class, and of the bourgeois State; they are daily and hourly enslaved by the machine, by the over-looker, and, above all, by the individual bourgeois manufacturer himself." In this regard, the liberal-democratic hypocrisy is not lost upon them, as they describe said "bondage" as the "autocratic power" of the capitalist, who acts without any respect for the otherwise esteemed "division of responsibility" and the "representative system."[27]

---

[25] Marx, *Economic Manuscript of 1861-63*, *MECW* 34: 122.
[26] Ibid., 411–412, 490, 474.
[27] Marx and Engels, *Manifesto of the Communist Party*, 49, 487.

The use of machinery also requires that the worker is drilled to act "as a machine,"[28] or a "living appendage of machine," as Marx rephrases it in *Capital*.[29] The worker's activity is here reduced to simple, one-sided and monotonous movements, and not the free, all-round activity befitting his/her human nature. Thus, Marx maintains that "the breaking up of the multifariousness of his employment"[30] turn the worker into a "crippled ... mere fragment of a man."[31] Again, this predicament of the worker is mediated by the worker's own creations.

These comments from the *Manifesto* and *Capital* echo Marx's following comments, found in the *Manuscripts of 1844*: "The machine accommodates itself to the *weakness* of the human being in order to make the *weak* human being into a machine."[32] Therefore, the forces of production are not the "free manifestations" of the workers, as *The German Ideology* also repeats.[33] In every turn, alienation thus comes to signify loss of control or freedom and, with that, of something that informs what it means to be human.

2.4 Social Alienation

How social alienation comes about is a complex matter, for it entails the other forms of alienation. Marx puts it thus:

> We must bear in mind ... that man's relation to himself becomes for him *objective* and *actual* through his relation to other men. Thus, if the product of his labor, his labor objectified, is for him an *alien, hostile,* powerful object independent of him, then his position towards it is such that someone else is the master of this object, someone who is alien, hostile, powerful, and independent of him. If he treats his own activity as an unfree activity, then he treats it as an activity performed in the service, under the dominion, the coercion, and the yoke of another man.[34]

---

[28] Ibid., 501.
[29] Marx, *Capital*, Vol. 1, 487.
[30] Ibid., 488.
[31] Ibid., 490.
[32] Marx, *Economic and Philosophic Manuscripts of 1844*, 308.
[33] Marx and Engels, *The German Ideology*, 438–39.
[34] Marx, *Economic and Philosophic Manuscripts of 1844*, 278–79.

According to Marx, therefore, a necessary relationship exists between different forms of alienation. To repeat,

> through estranged [alienated] labor man not only creates his relationship to the object and to the act of production as to powers ... that are alien and hostile to him; he also creates the relationship in which other men stand to his production and to his product, and the relationship in which he stands to these other men. Just as he creates his own production as the loss of his reality, as his punishment; his own product as a loss, as a product not belonging to him; so he creates the domination of the person who does not produce over production and over the product. Just as he estranges his own activity from himself, so he confers upon the stranger an activity which is not his own.[35]

An immediate "consequence of the fact that man is estranged from the product of his labor, from his life activity, from his species-being, is the *estrangement of man from man*."[36] Marx expresses this alienation-complex in a more digestible manner in *Capital*:

> [T]he the laborer ... is ... a source of wealth, but devoid of all means of making that wealth his own. Since, before entering on the process, his own labor has already been alienated from himself by the sale of his labor power, has been appropriated by the capitalist and incorporated with capital, it must, during the process, be realized in a product that does not belong to him. Since the process of production is also the process by which the capitalist consumes labor-power, the product of the laborer is incessantly converted, not only into commodities, but into capital, into value that sucks up the value-creating power, into means of subsistence that buy the person of the laborer, into means of production that command the producers. The laborer therefore constantly produces material, objective wealth, but in the form of capital, of an alien power that dominates and exploits him; and the capitalist as constantly produces labor power, but in the form of a subjective source of wealth, separated from the objects in and by which it can alone be realized; in short he produces the laborer, but as a wage

---

[35] Ibid., 279.
[36] Ibid., 277.

laborer. This incessant reproduction, this perpetuation of the laborer, is the *sine quâ non* of capitalist production.[37]

All this is made possible by "the capitalist ... command over the means of subsistence," including workers. Otherwise put, the "concentration of large masses of the means of production in the hands of individual capitalists is a material condition for the cooperation of the wage laborers." But, Marx reminds us, this is not sufficient: "All combined labor on a large scale requires, more or less, a directing authority, in order to secure the harmonious working of the individual activities."[38] This dominion of persons over persons is one important aspect of social alienation.

This social alienation applies to both workers and capitalists, for they represent the two sides of the same *human* alienation. In his wording, "The propertied class and the class of proletariat present the same human self-estrangement," though the former "recognizes estrangement *as its own power* and has in it the *semblance* of a human existence. The latter, feels annihilated in estrangement; it sees in it its own powerlessness and the reality of an inhuman existence.[39] The capitalist mode of production also engenders the alienation of workers from each other ("the laborers are isolated persons, who enter into [productive] relations with the capitalist, but not with one another").

A second, related aspect of it is inherent in the fact that "the co-operation of wage laborers is entirely brought about by the capital that employs them." This is an illusory productive community:

> Their union into one single productive body and the establishment of a connection between their individual functions are matters foreign and external to them, are not their own act, but the act of the capital that brings and keeps them together. Hence the connection existing between their various labors appears to them, ideally, in the shape of a preconceived plan of the capitalist, and practically in the shape of the authority of the same capitalist, who subjects their activity to his aims.[40]

---

[37] Marx, *Capital*, Vol. 1, 570–71.
[38] Ibid., 335–37.
[39] Marx and Engels, *The Holy Family*, 36.
[40] Ibid., 336–37.

This passage describes various forms of alienation, stressing social alienation:

> Being independent of each other, the laborers are isolated persons, who enter into relations with the capitalist, but not with one another. This cooperation begins only with the labor-process, but they have then ceased to belong to themselves ... As co-operators, as members of a working organism, they are but special modes of existence of capital.[41]

In short, as Leszek Kolakowski notes, Marx thinks the organization of the isolated individuals is "a technological process, not a human one."[42] If so, this process creates social cooperation and cohesion that somewhat paradoxically smack of isolation (alienation) of the naturally-social individuals from one another.

2.5 Alienation from the Species

Species-alienation includes all forms of alienation, including social alienation, since it generally refers to alienation from human essence. However, Marx often identifies it with one of its manifestations: "egotism," which will be our focus in this section.

As species-beings, individuals are other-regarding. In capitalist production, however, each satisfies the needs of others incidentally, that is, as a consequence of attempting to satisfy his/her own interests and needs.[43] "In bourgeois society," Marx argues in the *Grundrisse*, each tries to make a meal of [the community]," which in turn "makes a meal of him."[44] As we will see in due course, he frequently refers to this situation as "*bellum omnium contra omnes*," an expression borrowed from Hobbes.

Otherwise put, the processes of alienation "changes for him the *life of the species* into a means of individual life. First it estranges the life of the species and individual life, and secondly it makes individual life in its abstract [one-sided] form the purpose of the life

---

[41] Ibid., 338.

[42] Kolakowski, *Main Currents of Marxism,* Vol. 1, 286.

[43] Marx, *Outlines of the Critique of Political Economy* (*Grundrisse*), *MECW* 28: 174-75.

[44] Ibid., 420. As we will see in the next chapter, Marx regards this as species alienation.

of the species, likewise in its abstract and estranged form." Thus, the isolated, egotistical individual becomes the end of the community in its alienated form (i.e., in bourgeois society). According to Marx, "estranged labor" is the ultimate basis of this individualistic turn, for it converts *"man's species-being* [read community] ... into a being *alien* to him, into a *means* for his *individual existence*."[45]

Two aspects of Marx's explanation of this egotism should be further stressed. The first aspect has to do with how individuals are conditioned by the processes of alienation to define the purpose of their productive activity in capitalism:

> I have produced for myself and not for you, just as you have produced for yourself and not for me ... That is ..., our production is ... not *social* production [and so is inconsistent with the individual's social essence] ... For it is not man's nature that forms the link between the products we make for one another ... [Consequently,] each of us sees in his product only the objectification of his own selfish need, and therefore in the product of the other the objectification of a different selfish need, independent of him and alien to him.[46]

After belaboring this issue from all sorts of angles, Marx concludes that, in this process, "Our *mutual* value is for us the *value* of our mutual objects. Hence for us man himself is mutually of *no value*." Typically, he contrasts this form of alienation with a speculatively conceived communistic scenario in which the social nature of production is presupposed and, with that, each freely and consciously produces (also) for the sake of others, to satisfy their needs. If this were to exist, says Marx, "I would have directly confirmed and realized my true nature, my *human* nature, my *communal* nature,"[47] and so would have acted in accordance with my species essence.

Marx here agrees and disagrees with Adam Smith.[48] He agrees with the latter's depiction of the purpose of production in a

---

[45] Marx, *Economic and Philosophic Manuscripts of 1844*, 276-77.
[46] Ibid., 225.
[47] Ibid., 226-27.
[48] Marx quotes some parts of the following paragraph from Smith in the *Manuscripts of 1844*, 317-18.

capitalistic economy. According to Smith, "It is not from the benevolence of the butcher, the brewer, or the baker that we expect our dinner, but from their regard to their own interest. We address ourselves, not to their humanity but to their self-love, and never talk to them of our own necessities but of their advantages." Of course, "we" are also producers in some form and capacity, including being wage workers, and so act, in this capacity too, in accordance with our own interests, regarding others as means to our aims.[49] The disagreement emerges from Smith's (somewhat reluctant) attribution of this egotism to human nature. Marx, on the other hand, regards it as a form of historically produced species-alienation.

Marx's definition of exploitation in *The German Ideology* as deriving "benefit for myself by doing harm to someone else" entails this aspect of alienation. Marx and Engels also associate exploitation with the bourgeois conception of utility, which demands products of utility from "each ability … alien to it."[50]

A second articulation of egotism has more to do with the buying and selling of commodities—as opposed to the purpose of producing them. "Under [the system of] private property," Marx argues, "every person speculates on creating a *new* need in another, so as to drive him to fresh sacrifice, to place him in a new dependence and to seduce him into a new mode of *enjoyment* and therefore economic ruin. Consequently, "each tries to establish over the other an *alien* power, so as thereby to find satisfaction of his own selfish need." This is nothing short of "mutual swindling and mutual plundering. Man becomes ever poorer as man" as a result.[51]

In bourgeois society, Marx stresses more generally in *Capital,* the main force that brings the individuals

in relation with each other [in the sphere of exchange] is the selfishness, the gain and the private interests of each. Each looks to himself only, and no one troubles himself about the rest, and just because they do so, do they all, in accordance with pre-established harmony of things, or under the auspices of all-shrewd providence, work together to their mutual

---

[49] Smith, *An Inquiry into the Nature and Causes of the Wealth of Nations*, Bk. 1, Ch. 2.

[50] Marx and Engels, *The German Ideology*, 409–10.

[51] Marx, *Economic and Philosophic Manuscripts of 1844*, 307.

advantage, for the common weal and in the interest of all.[52]

It is worth reiterating once more that this alienated figure, whose selfish, instrumentalist treatment of others also expresses his/her own *human* impoverishment, constitutes the "universal" standpoint of Marx's ideological opponents: "*Society,* as it appears to the political economist, is *civil society* in which every individual is a totality of needs and only exists for the other person, as the other exists for him, insofar as each becomes a means for the other."[53] These are the very "economists who obliterate all historical differences and see bourgeois relations in all forms of society."[54] For Marx, as we have also seen in the previous chapter, what the political economist, as well as the likes of Feuerbach, takes to be the natural (or universal) individuality is actually a historical result.[55] However, I argue, his own account of historical differences should not be reduced to an account of such differences alone. Instead, it is also meant to reveal what differentiates "bourgeois relations" from *human* relations, and so to determine how these amount to alienation.

***

The material presented above, much of which is drawn from Marx's "mature" works, to borrow Ernest Mandel's expression, "reduces to ashes the thesis defended" by Althusser and many others—that Marx had abandoned the theory of alienation in his later works.[56] As far as I am concerned, this specific issue is now settled, meaning that the presence of the theory of alienation, and of human nature, in Marx's later oeuvre will be taken for granted in the ensuing chapters of the present study.

The sustained presence of the theory of alienation in Marx's oeuvre raises other important questions, however: Does his theory of alienation imply a moral (or normative) critique of capitalism? What is the relationship between his theory of alienation and his

---

[52] Marx, *Capital*, Vol. 1, 186.

[53] Ibid., 317.

[54] Marx, *Outlines of the Critique of Political Economy*, *MECW* 28: 42. Translation slightly edited.

[55] Marx, *Economic and Philosophic Manuscripts of 1844*, 307.

[56] Mandel, *The Formation of the Economic Thought of Karl Marx*, 177.

vision of revolution and communism? These questions, along with other related questions, will be answered in the subsequent chapters. The next chapter attempts to explain how the theory of alienation significantly informs Marx's famous formulation(s) of the structure-superstructure nexus.

Alienation and the State

3.1 Introduction

The importance of the theory of alienation to Marx's understanding of the state has been seldom noticed. Following Paul Thomas, "The point here is not simply that what I am calling 'alien politics' is an integral part of Marx's theory of the state; it is also that there are connections—connections important to an understanding of Marx's enterprise in general—between Marx's theory of the state and Marx's theory of alienation."[1] This chapter seeks to articulate several such connections.

3.2 briefly discusses the structure-superstructure nexus, as it was famously formulated by the mature Marx. Based on his various comments on it, it defines the two terms of the nexus, rather minimally, as social relations of production and juridical-political relations (i.e., the state) respectively. It then posits the sense in which the nexus is informed by the theory of alienation, thus anticipating the themes of the subsequent sections of this chapter. 3.3 illustrates the repeated articulation of the nexus in Marx's early works, especially the ones in which the concept of the state is explicitly linked to alienation. The chief aim of 3.4 is to illustrate the consistency between Marx's class- and alienation-theory of the state. 3.5 documents his derivation of the most fundamental bourgeois right (law), namely, the right to private property, from the social relations of production and exchange, entailing alienation. This is retrieved from his mature economic works and is shown to dovetail his general formulation of the nexus.

Although the chapter may be read as a standalone essay, its primary purpose is to explain why Marx thought the state is inherently antithetical to freedom and sought to abolish it for this very reason. This issue, however, will be considered, especially, in Chapter 8.

---

[1] Thomas, *Karl Marx and the Anarchists*. Also see Thomas, *Alien Politics*; Sayer, "The Critique of Politics and Political Economy: Capitalism, Communism, and the State in Marx's Writings of the Mid-1840s," 221-53. For a brief, yet rich and clear, survey of various Marxist theories of the state, see Das, "Marxist Theories of the State."

3.2 The Structure-Superstructure Nexus

Let us begin with the most well-known passage in which Marx mentions the nexus:

> In the social production of their existence, men inevitably enter into definite relations ..., namely relations of production appropriate to a given stage in the development of their material forces of production. The totality of these relations of production constitutes the economic structure of society, the real foundation, on which arises a legal and political superstructure and to which correspond definite forms of social consciousness.[2]

Despite the enormous amount of thinking and writing that went into the analysis of this issue, there is no consensus on what sort of determination, arising, or corresponding Marx had in mind in this and other related passages.[3] The most prevalent view has it that the economic structure is *causally* prioritized in the nexus, and this in an exaggerated way, which renders the state (or politics in general) merely an epiphenomenon of things economic. This interpretation is not without merit, though it is itself an exaggeration.[4]

Leaving this issue aside, it is worth noting that Marx here equates the structure of a society with its social relations of production, and its superstructure with its "legal and political" relations, *excluding* "forms of social consciousness" (ideology, etc.)

---

[2] Marx, *Outlines of the Critique of Political Economy*, 263.

[3] For a very interesting and informed treatment of the "biography" of the nexus, see Dileep Edara, *Biography of a Blunder: Base and Superstructure in Marx and Later*.

[4] Engels: "If some younger writers attribute more importance to the economic aspect than is its due, Marx and I are to some extent to blame," adding that they "had to stress this leading principle in the face of opponents who denied it, and we did not always have the time, space and opportunity to do justice to the other factors that interacted upon each other." However, Engels goes on to point out how Marx, often enough, gave causal significance to politics in his various works, such as *Eighteenth Brumaire* and *Capital*, and asks rhetorically: "Or why then do we fight for the political dictatorship of the proletariat, if political power is economically powerless?" "Engels to Joseph Bloch, September 21-22, 1890," 34–36.

from the superstructure.[5] His comment on this well-known passage in the first volume of *Capital* basically repeats the same, somewhat vague, definitions.[6]

I think the clearest reiteration of the nexus, as it applies to capitalism, is given in the third volume of *Capital*:

> The specific economic form, in which unpaid surplus-labor is pumped out of direct producers, determines the relationship of rulers and ruled, as it grows directly out of production itself and, in turn, reacts upon it as a determining element ... It is always the direct relationship of the owners of the conditions [or means] of production to the direct producers ... which reveals the innermost secret, the hidden basis of the entire social structure and with it the political form of the relation of sovereignty and dependence, in short, the corresponding specific form of the state.[7]

To wit, the system of production based on wage labor gives you the most elemental social relations of the capitalist society, that between capitalists (rulers) and workers (ruled), as well as the most elemental property relations of this form of society. This is the *underlying* structure of all *capitalist* societies, to which corresponds a "specific form of the state."[8]

---

[5] It is reasonably clear that Marx was averse to providing precise definitions. As Engels puts it in his "Preface" the third volume of *Capital*, it is "false" to think that Marx "wishes to define where he only investigates, and that in general one might expect fixed, cut-to-measure, once and for all applicable definitions in Marx's works." Marx, *Capital*, Vol. 3, 16. For interesting discussions of this issue, see Ollman, *Alienation*, esp. Ch. 1; Sayer, *The Violence of Abstraction*. For my own musings on this issue, see Tabak, *Dialectics of Human Nature in Marx's Philosophy*, Ch. 3.

[6] Marx, *Capital*, Vol. 1, 92–93, n. 1.

[7] Marx, *Capital*, Vol. 3, 777-78.

[8] To further clarify, its presence in different societies "does not prevent the same economic basis [structure]—the same from the standpoint of its main conditions— ... from showing infinite variations and gradations in appearance, which can be ascertained only by analysis of the empirically given circumstances." Such variations, he writes, are due to "tradition ..., innumerable different empirical circumstances, natural environment, racial relations, external historical influences, etc." (ibid., 778-79). Also see

Alienation and the State

I now posit that the theory of alienation is implicated in this nexus. Briefly put, the structural relations Marx describes above are precisely the alienated production and property relations in capitalist society (see Chapter 2). The ensuing sections illustrate this claim in some detail.

3.3 The Origins of the Nexus

In his "Preface" to *A Contribution to the Critique of Political Economy*, Marx states that the "guiding principle" of his intellectual inquiries, which contains the nexus, was first articulated in an essay he published in *Deutsch–Französische Jahrbücher* (1844),[9] namely, the *Contribution to the Critique of Hegel's Philosophy of Law: Introduction*. Thus, by his own admission, the nexus was first formulated by the *young* Marx.

"The immediate *task of philosophy*," Marx asserts in that article, "is to unmask self-estrangement in its *unholy forms* ..., once the *holy form* of human self-estrangement has been unmasked ... Thus..., the *criticism of religion* [turns] into the *criticism of law,* and the *criticism of theology* into the *criticism of politics.*"[10] In a nutshell, Marx's main task in this essay is to "unmask self-estrangement" entailed in the "*law*" and "*politics.*" Otherwise put, he claims that the modern state, much exalted by Hegel as an expression of freedom, is directly linked to—or rather reflects—social relations of alienation "in which man is a debased, enslaved, abandoned, despicable" being.[11]

Marx's "On the Jewish Question," also published in the *Deutsch-Französische Jahrbücher*, explores this issue in more detail. This essay is framed as a rebuttal of Bruno Bauer's claim—here put in a nutshell—that freedom consists in becoming citizens

---

Marx, *Critique of the Gotha Program*, 94. As Ellen M. Wood puts it, this "means, first of all, that we cannot simply read off the empirical specificities of any given society from its economic 'base'; but it also means that the logic of the economic basis is discernible throughout those empirical manifestations." Wood, "Historical Materialism in 'Forms which Precede Capitalist Production'," 90.

[9] Marx, *Outlines of the Critique of Political Economy*, 262.
[10] Marx, "Contribution to the Critique of Hegel's Philosophy of Law: Introduction," 176.
[11] Ibid., 182.

30

of the "modern," so-called "free," state. One of the central tenets of Marx's critique of Bauer is that he fails to realize how political emancipation does not amount to full *human* emancipation.[12] *Inter alia*, Marx consequently focuses on explaining how the modern state can at most reflect abstract freedom, mainly defined as membership of individuals in an illusory community. In the modern state, he writes accordingly, "man frees himself through the *medium of the state* ... in a *roundabout way*."[13]

Put another way, as citizens, individuals are members of an "illusory" community, and so are abstractly free in this sense. In the meanwhile, "All the preconditions of ... egoistic [and antagonistic] life continue to exist in *civil society outside* the sphere of the state, but as qualities of civil society." If so—and here comes a formulation of the structure-superstructure nexus, "Far from abolishing these real distinctions, the state only exists on the presupposition of their existence; it feels itself to be a political state and asserts its universality only in opposition to these [particularistic] elements of its being." "Only in this way, *above* the *particular* elements," Marx continues, "does the state constitute itself as universality."[14]

These observations underpin Marx's famous image of the "twofold life" in bourgeois society, which is also an image of the structure-superstructure nexus:

> Where the political state has attained its true development, man—not only in thought, in consciousness, but in reality, in life—leads a twofold life, a heavenly and an earthly life: life in the political community, in which he considers himself a communal being, and life in civil society, in which he acts as a private individual, regards other men as a means, degrades himself into a means, and becomes the plaything of alien powers.[15]

In the modern "free-state," Marx goes on to add, every individual merely formally or abstractly "ranks as *sovereign,* as the

---

[12] Marx, "On the Jewish Question," 149.
[13] Ibid., 152.
[14] Ibid.
[15] Ibid., 154.

highest being," whereas in real life he is found "in his uncivilized, unsocial form, man in his fortuitous existence, man just as he is, man as he has been corrupted by the whole organization of our society, who has lost himself, been alienated, and handed over to the rule of inhuman conditions and elements—in short, man who is not yet a *real* species-being."[16]

Marx's imagery of the life in "civil society" here dovetails the theory of alienation he contemporaneously developed in the *Manuscripts of 1844*. In other words, it should not be controversial to claim that he presupposes the four aspects of the alienation-complex (see Chapter 2) in his depiction of "civil society" in "On the Jewish Question," though his emphasis here is on the alienation (isolation and egotism) of individuals from their species-essence. He describes this aspect of alienation as—and as usual—the "sphere of egoism, of *bellum omnium contra omnes*." This statement basically characterizes the nature of the *structure* of bourgeois society, to which necessarily corresponds the alien state (superstructure). So, the nexus between them is put thus: The modern state "has become the expression of man's *separation* from his *community, from himself and from other men.*"[17] Reversely restated, "This *man*, the member of civil society, is thus the basis, the precondition, of the *political* state. He is recognized as such by this state in the rights of man."[18]

"None of the so-called rights of man," Marx goes on to argue,

> go beyond egoistic man, beyond man as a member of civil society, that is, an individual withdrawn into himself, into the confines of his private interests and private caprice, and separated from the community. In the rights of man, he is far from being conceived as a species-being; on the contrary, species-like itself, society, appears as a framework external to the individuals, as a restriction of their original independence.[19]

Marx's wholesale reduction of "the rights of man," inscribed in

---

[16] Ibid., 159.
[17] Ibid., 154-55.
[18] Ibid., 166.
[19] Ibid., 164.

the "Declaration of the Rights of Man and of the Citizen," to "the rights of egoistic man" is difficult to justify.[20] Be this as it may, his critique of "the rights of man" mainly focuses on the right to private property. "The sole bond holding them together is natural necessity, need and private interest, the preservation of their property and their egoistic selves," he stresses in this regard.[21] A quick look at the *Manuscripts of 1844* (see Chapter 2) would reveal that he thinks this right issues from the alienated relations of production. We will see in the last section of this chapter how this view is also defended in his mature *economic* works.

In another article from this period, Marx expresses the structure-superstructure nexus in a single sentence: "The existence of the state and the existence of slavery are inseparable."[22] In this article, the nexus between slavery (alienation) and the state is explicitly understood as the structure-superstructure nexus: "The *present structure of society*" is "the *principle of the state*." The state, he adds accordingly, is "the official expression" of antagonistic society, in which "social maladies" (or estrangement in general) are rampant.[23]

Marx continues the same polemic against Bauer in *The Holy Family* (1845), claiming that "it was demonstrated to Herr Bauer" in "On the Jewish Question" that the so-called "'free humanity' and the [political] 'recognition of it are nothing but the recognition of the *egoistic civil individual*," belonging to "*present-day* civil life," and that "the *rights of man* ... procure for him [only] *freedom of property*." Consequently, rather than freeing "him from the filth of

---

[20] As Lefort puts it, "Marx sees in the freedom of action and the freedom of opinion granted to everyone, and in the guarantees of individual security, no more than the establishment of a new model which enshrines 'the separation of man from man' or, at a more basic level still, 'bourgeois egotism.'" Lefort, *Democracy and Political Theory*, 32. Similarly, Lukes protests: "To think of [all rights] merely as expressing the egoism of civil society and the contradictions between civil society and the state is precisely to fail to take them seriously." Such failure cannot see the seriousness of demanding "a certain form of social life in which social relationships flourish free of arbitrary political power." Lukes, *Marxism and Morality*, 65.
[21] Marx, "On the Jewish Question," 164.
[22] Marx, "Critical Marginal Notes on the Article 'The King of Prussia and Social Reform' by a Prussian," 198.
[23] Ibid., 199.

gain," they "give him *freedom of gainful occupation*."[24] Rather than true freedom, retorts Marx with a dose of rhetorical exaggeration, "It was shown [to Bauer] that the *recognition of the rights of man* by the *modern state*" resembles "the *recognition of slavery* by the *state of antiquity*." Once more, this resemblance is explicitly articulated in terms of the base- or structure-superstructure nexus:

> [J]ust as the ancient state had [the society based on] slavery as its *natural basis*, the *modern state* has as its *natural basis* civil society and the *man* of civil society, i.e., the independent [alienated, isolated] man linked with other men only by the ties of private interest and *unconscious* natural necessity, the *slave* of labor for gain and of his own as well as other men's *selfish* need.[25]

Marx repeats the same argument, as well as the same comparison of the ancient and modern systems of slavery, in *Capital*, as we will see in 3.5. Moreover, he here, as elsewhere, uses the word "slavery" in two different senses. One of them is the less familiar sense, related to selfishness, which denotes succumbing to one's egotistical urges and interests. The second sense has to do with the domination of the worker by the capitalist. Thus, the term "slavery" denotes both the alienation of individuals from their species-essence and their alienation as the kind of unfreedom expressed in the antagonistic relationship in which one class dominates the other. All this is summed up thus: The modern state (superstructure) "is based on *emancipated slavery, bourgeois society* ..., [which is] the society of industry, of universal competition, of private interest freely following its aims, of anarchy, of the self-estranged natural and spiritual individuality."[26]

In short, the modern state reflects the alienated relations in bourgeois society. In addition, Marx assumes that the state also preserves these relations, thus suggesting that the superstructure is both determined and determining. This conclusion will be further reiterated in the next section, in which we will also discover a remarkable affinity between Marx's alienation-theory of the state

---

[24] Marx and Engels, *The Holy Family*, 113.
[25] Ibid.
[26] Ibid., 122.

and the more well-known class-theory of the state. We will also discover the alien state as a top-down political power, which is also detectable in Marx's earlier writings.

3.4 Autonomy of the State

The German Ideology, which is known to emphasize the class-theory of the state, also repeats the key tenets of the alienation-theory of the state. For instance, it claims that "civil law develops simultaneously [not temporally after!] with private property out of the disintegration of the natural community." Put from another angle, "because individuals seek *only* their particular interest ..., common interest ... is asserted as an interest 'alien' to them, and 'independent' of them." At the same time, "the *practical* struggle of these particular interests, which *actually* constantly run counter to the common and illusory common interests, necessitates *practical* intervention and restraint through the illusory 'general' interest in the form of the state."[27]

The same thought is repeated in the same text, though this time with an explicit reference to class domination:

> Out of this very contradiction between the particular and the common interests, the common interest assumes an independent form as the *state*, which is divorced from the real individual and collective interests, and at the same time as an illusory community, always based, however, on the existing real ties [i.e., social relations of production] ..., especially ..., on the classes, already implied by the division of labor, which in every such mass of men separate out, and one [class] of which dominates all the others.[28]

This passage expresses, or else implies, four things that endorse the main claims of this chapter. First, it is generally about the structure-superstructure nexus. Second, this nexus is informed by the theory of alienation. Third, the claim that the state in question "is divorced from the real individual and collective interests" implies not only that the state is "independent" of society in some sense but also that, by the same token, it is not a free expression of

---

[27] Marx and Engels, *The German Ideology*, 90.
[28] Ibid., 46–47.

its denizens, for it rules them from above. Fourth, Marx himself assumes that the alienation- and the class-theory of the state dovetail each other.

I suggest that what matters ultimately in establishing the compatibility of the two theories is their content, and not whether the word "alienation" is explicitly used. Thus, I assume that Marx's following claim in the "materialist" *The Poverty of Philosophy* repeats the logic of the alienation-theory of the state, as well as the structure-superstructure nexus entailed therein: "Political power is precisely the official expression of antagonism [*bellum omnium contra omnes*] in civil society."[29]

It might be objected that the *Manifesto* proposes the class-theory of the state *simpliciter*, which is also known as the "tool-state" theory. After all, it famously states: "The executive of the modern state is but [or only] a committee for managing the common affairs of the whole bourgeoisie."[30] This statement appears to deny at least one of the crucial implications of the alienation-theory of the state, namely, the autonomy of the state. Yet, and contrary to a very popular view on this issue, the "tool state" we encounter here is an exception, not the norm.

The autonomy of the state, *The German Ideology* argues, is even found in the in the United States (the "most perfect" bourgeois state), where "the state has become a separate entity, beside and outside civil society." Such a state, Marx and Engels clarify, is "the form of organization which the bourgeois necessarily adopt both for internal and external purposes, for the mutual guarantee of their property and interests."[31] If so, there is an inherent link between the alienated-antagonistic society and the relative *autonomy* of the state.

Unlike France and, especially, Germany, Marx repeats in the *Grundrisse*, in the United States, "the bourgeois society is not

---

[29] Marx, *The Poverty of Philosophy*, 212.

[30] Marx and Engels, *Manifesto of the Communist Party*, 486. The last, often-quoted sentence speaks of the relationship between state authority or power (*moderne Staatsgewalt*) and the bourgeoisie, the ruling class, which is commonly translated as the "executive power." Indeed, the original of the sentence *does* assert that this (executive) power is "only" or "merely" (or *nothing but*) a committee (*ist nur ein Ausschuß...*) for managing the common affairs of the entire bourgeoisie.

[31] Marx and Engels, *The German Ideology*, 90.

developing on the basis of feudalism but in which it has originated from itself ... the state, in contradistinction from all earlier national forms, was from the start subordinated to bourgeois society, to its production, and could never make the claim of being an end in itself." Yet, even "in North America ..., the power of the central government grows with the centralization of capital."[32]

The logic behind this assumption is articulated in Marx's and Engels' review of Emile de Girardin's *Le socialisme et l'impôt*: "The bourgeois state is ... the mutual insurance of the bourgeois class against its individual members, as well as the exploited class, insurance which will necessarily become increasingly expensive and to all appearances increasingly independent of bourgeois society."[33]

Thus, the autonomy or the "independence" of the state is a necessary function of the multi-level antagonisms in bourgeois society. Since these antagonisms are essential aspects of the structure of bourgeois society, it follows, according to the logic of the structure-superstructure nexus, that the autonomy of the state is also its essential feature. The same logic issues from the equation of these antagonisms with the general division of labor in capitalism.

Marx also frequently focuses on the autonomy of the state in his political writings on French politics, consistently stressing its bureaucratic-autocratic power and self-interested control over the entire society. By the same token, he maintains that the bourgeoisie necessarily supports (or had adopted in France) the bureaucratic state, limiting its own aspirations to rule directly via the liberal-democratic parliament. Thus, in the *Brumaire*, he argues that "in order to preserve its social power intact, its political power must be broken [or abdicated to the bureaucratic state]; that the individual bourgeois can continue to exploit the other classes and to enjoy undisturbed property, family, religion and order only on condition that their class be condemned along with the other classes to similar political nullity."[34]

In short, and to repeat, bourgeois society necessary gives way to the autonomy of the state, specifically, to its bureaucratic

[32] Marx, *Outlines of the Critique of Political Economy*, *MECW* 28: 6-7.
[33] Marx and Engels, "*Le socialisme et l'impôt, par Émile de Girardin*," 333.
[34] Marx, *The Eighteenth Brumaire of Louis Bonaparte*, 142-43.

executive power, though the level and form of its autonomy varies in different societies. As Engels explains,

> The state ... is the admission that [bourgeois] society has ... split into irreconcilable opposites which it is powerless to dispel. But in order that these opposites, classes with conflicting economic interests, might not consume themselves and society in fruitless struggle, it became necessary to have a power seemingly standing above society which would alleviate the conflict and keep it within the bounds of "order"; and this power, having arisen out of society but placing itself above it, and alienating itself more and more from it, is the state.[35]

3.5 Alienation and the State in *Capital* and Its Drafts

Although they are not usually known for this, *Capital* and Marx's other "mature" economic writings contain some of his most interesting comments on the state. This section focuses on his comments on a fundamental moment of the capitalist state, namely, the right (law) to private property and the nexus between social alienation and the autonomy of the state.

In "The Value-Form," Marx posits that *"products of labor* would not become commodities, were they not products of separate *private labors* carried on independently of one another."[36] As we have seen in Chapter 2, the concept and practice of "private labors" is predicated upon commodified labor power of the isolated producers ("separate *private labors*"), and the constant sale-exchange of this power is an essential precondition for the constant conversion of products into commodities and of their transfer to the capitalist.

As Marx explains in *Capital*, "labor-power can appear upon the market as a commodity only if, and so far as, its possessor, the individual whose labor-power it is, offers it for sale, or sells it, as a commodity. In order that he may be able to do this, he must ... be [recognized as] the untrammeled owner of his capacity for labor, i.e., of his person."[37] "The capitalist epoch," Marx goes on to further

---

[35] Engels, *Origin of the Family, Private Property, and State*, 269.

[36] Marx, "The Value-Form," 131-33.

[37] Marx, *Capital*, Vol. 1, 178.

clarify, is "characterized by the fact that labor-power, [even] in the eyes of the worker himself, takes on the form of a commodity which is his property; his labor consequently takes on the form of wage-labor."[38] The whole thing significantly hinges on recognition.

Marx maintains here that the capitalistic form of private property issues from the alienation (sale) of a person's "capacity for labor," and so entails self-alienation. In order to drive this very point home, he footnotes the following paragraph from Hegel's *Philosophy of Right*:

> "I may [alienate] ... to another the use, for a limited time, of my particular bodily and mental aptitudes and capabilities ... But by the alienation of all my labor-time and the whole of my work, I should be converting the substance itself, in other words, my general activity and reality, my person, into the property of another."[39]

Unlike Hegel, however, Marx is troubled by both wage-slavery and its legalization by the state. Thus, he points out approvingly, when "the so-called Emperor Maximilian re-established [wage-labor] by a decree," "the House of Representatives at Washington ... *aptly* denounced [it] as a decree for the re-introduction of slavery into Mexico [emphasis added]."[40] This will of the state also entails legalizing the commodification of persons.[41]

To recapitulate, Marx maintains that alienated labor is the ground of what the liberal philosophers regard as natural rights of individuals to private property. In *Capital*, he describes this situation colorfully, and with a dose of sarcasm, thus:

> This sphere ..., within whose boundaries the sale and purchase of labor-power goes on, is in fact a very Eden of the [so-called] innate rights of man. There alone rule Freedom, Equality, Property and Bentham. Freedom, because both buyer and seller of a commodity, say of labor-power, are constrained

---

[38] Ibid, 180 n. 1.
[39] Ibid., 178 n. 2. Hegel, *Elements of the Philosophy of Right*, 97 (§ 67).
[40] Marx, *Capital*, Vol. 1, 178, n. 2.
[41] Quoting Hobbes: "'The value or work of a man, is as of all other things his price—that is to say, as much as would be given for the use of his power.'" Ibid, 180 n. 2. See Hobbes, *Leviathan*, 59.

only by their own free will. They contract as free agents, and the agreement they come to, is but the form in which they give legal expression to their common will. Equality, because each enters into relation with the other, as with a simple owner of commodities, and they exchange equivalent for equivalent. Property, because each disposes only of what is his own. And Bentham, because each looks only to himself.[42]

However, something else lurks behind this much-exalted freedom and equality, according to Marx. The following comparison brings it into sharp relief: "The Roman slave was held by fetters; the wage laborer is bound to his owner by invisible threads. The appearance of independence is kept up by means of a constant change of employers, and by the *fictio juris* of a contract," which is itself based on the double-principle of freedom (free will) and equality of the contracting persons.[43] If so, and once again, a slave-like relationship exists between the worker and the capitalist within the sphere of production, which is what lurks behind "equality" and "freedom."[44] What we now have, therefore, is an internally related double-relationship: freedom in the sphere of exchange and a modern form of slavery in that of production.

Elsewhere, Marx creatively explains what goes on in these two spheres in terms of "two acts." "The first act fully corresponds to the laws of commodity circulation, to which it belongs. Equivalents are exchanged for equivalents" between the capitalist and the worker. From this vantage point, or in this act, we discover what appears to be capitalism's most elementary relationship, the relationship "individuals enter with each other ... [as rightful]

---

[42] Marx, *Capital*, Vol. 1, 186.

[43] Ibid., 573.

[44] "On leaving the sphere of simple circulation or of exchange of commodities, which furnishes the 'Free-trader Vulgaris' with his views and ideas, and with the standard by which he judges a society based on capital and wages," writes Marx playfully, we think we can perceive a change in the physiognomy of our dramatis personae. He, who before was the money owner [in the act of purchasing labor power], now [in the sphere of production] strides in front as capitalist; the possessor of labor-power follows as his laborer. The one with an air of importance, smirking, intent on business; the other, timid and holding back, like one who is bringing his own hide to market and has nothing to expect but—a hiding" (ibid., 186).

commodity owners." However, an entirely different scenario emerges in "the second act," which contradicts the first:

> In the first place, the social position of the seller and the buyer changes in the production process itself. The buyer takes command of the seller, to the extent that the latter himself enters into the buyer's consumption process with his person as a worker. There comes into being, outside the simple exchange process, a relation of domination and servitude, [which] ... therefore in itself ... includes political, etc., relationships.[45]

Since the ideological standpoint of bourgeois society is based on the first act, all it reveals is the abstract, formal equality and freedom of individuals, which then take on a legal, juridical form.[46] In addition to concealing the "slavery" entailed in this relation, which is basically the alienation of the worker from his or her activity, the same standpoint also "mystifies" exploitation: "This is owing to the fact, first, that the capital which is exchanged for labor power is itself but a portion of the products of others' labor appropriated without an equivalent; and, secondly, that this capital must not only be replaced by its producer, but replaced together with an added surplus."[47] Thus, "what really takes place is this—the capitalist again and again appropriates, without an equivalent, a portion of the previously materialized labor of others, and exchanges it for a greater quantity of living labor."[48] Now the "legal relation," based on "equality and freedom," turns out to be "a *deceptive appearance.*"[49]

Following this logic, Marx reiterates in the *Grundrisse* that "the private property in the product of one's own labor is identical with the separation of labor and property; as a result, one's labor will create someone else's property and property [expropriated by the capitalist] will command someone else's labor.[50] Thus, private

---

[45] Marx, *Economic Manuscript of 1861-63*, 105–06.
[46] Marx, *Outlines of the Critique of Political Economy*, *MECW* 29: 474–75.
[47] Marx, *Capital*, Vol. 1, 582.
[48] Ibid., 583.
[49] Marx, *A Contribution to the Critique of Political Economy*, *MECW* 28: 392.
[50] Ibid., 170.

property becomes the means with which the capitalist purchases, controls, and exploits the worker *legally*.

As Marx further articulates in *Capital*, "property turns out to be the right, on the part of the capitalist, to appropriate the unpaid labor of others or its product, and to be the impossibility, on the part of the laborer, of appropriating his own product. The separation of property from labor has become the necessary consequence of a law that apparently originated in their identity."[51] Therefore, and in the *Grundrisse* again,

> the right to property on the side of capital is transformed into the right of property in alien labor, the right to appropriate alien labor without equivalent; on the side of labor capacity, it is transformed into the duty to relate itself towards its own labor or its own product as *alien property*. The right to property is inverted into the right on the one side to appropriate alien labor and the duty on the other side to respect the product of one's own labor and one's own labor itself as values belonging to others.[52]

In *Capital*, as elsewhere, Marx also comments on the relationship between the exchange of commodities (products) and the legal-political superstructure corresponding to it. His assertoric attempt to explain the latter as the product or "reflex" of the "economic relations" of the parties involved is unsatisfactory. However, it does point to an important aspect of the alienation-theory of the state, namely, its autonomy. This stems from the (unoriginal) notion that the rights and freedoms of the exchanging parties, as well as their contractual relations, require legal and political guarantees.[53]

As Marx further explains in the same text, the antagonism among capitalists, which has its basis in the division of labor within the realm of production and "free competition" in the market, "brings out the inherent laws of capitalist production in the shape of external coercive laws having power over every individual

---

[51] Marx, *Capital*, Vol. 1, 582–83.
[52] Marx, *A Contribution to the Critique of Political Economy*, *MECW* 28: 386.
[53] Marx, *Capital,* Vol. 1, 95.

capitalist."[54] The upshot is that the economic society (structure) is a realm of social alienation, and so is an illusory community, which requires the autonomous state to maintain it. In this sense, and to requote the relevant passage from Marx's and Engels' review of Emile de Girardin's *Le socialisme et l'impôt*, "The bourgeois state is ... the mutual insurance of the bourgeois class against its individual members, as well as the exploited class, insurance which will necessarily become ... increasingly independent of bourgeois society."[55]

As Marx puts it more generally in the third volume of *Capital*, "regulation and order are themselves indispensable elements of any mode of production, if it is to assume social stability and independence from mere chance and arbitrariness. These are precisely the form of its social stability and therefore its relative freedom from mere arbitrariness and mere chance."[56] In other words, in bourgeois society, capitalists hold direct authority over workers through economic and politico-juridical means. However, "among the bearers of this authority, the capitalists themselves, who confront one another only as commodity-owners, there reigns complete anarchy within which the social interrelations of production assert themselves only as an overwhelming natural law in relation to individual free will."[57]

This structural anarchy (alienation) requires a "legal and political" superstructure to manage it, and to transfigure the antagonisms inherent therein into abstract "common interest." This, once again, requires the autonomy of the superstructure, that is, of the alien state. To wit, the invisible hand is puppeteered by a very visible one.

***

The alienation-theory of the state presented in this chapter bears important implications for Marx's practical philosophy of freedom. In a nutshell, the theory treats the state both as a reflection of unfreedom entailed in structural relations and as an autonomous

---

[54] Ibid., 276.
[55] Marx and Engels, "*Le socialisme et l'impôt, par Émile de Girardin*," 333.
[56] Marx, *Capital*, Vol. 3, 779–80.
[57] Ibid., 867.

entity that not only maintains such relations but also dominates society in a top-down manner. Thus, dealienation or emancipation requires more than the transcendence of the alienated social relations of production, for the state itself must also be abolished. We will see in Chapter 8 that Marx's vision of socialism entails the revolutionary abolition of the state—its replacement with expansive democracy, and this for reasons having to do with its link to unfreedom. However, several additional steps need to be taken beforehand. One of them is whether Marx's theory of alienation entails ethical judgement (Chapter 4), and the other is whether such a judgement grounds his justification of revolution (Chapter 5).

Critique of Alienation and Ethics

4.1 Introduction

Much has been written on whether Marx's assessment of capitalism entails ethical or moral judgement.[1] Every possible answer one can imagine, including the claims that he thought it was just (ethical), unjust (unethical), both, and neither, is found in the existing literature.[2] In this regard, this chapter defends the double-view that Marx was critical of ethical approaches—because they were *ethical*, but also consistently critiqued alienation on what *we* may call "ethical" grounds. Rather than attempting to resolve it—because I take it to be unresolvable, this chapter concludes that the latter horn of the dilemma is demonstrably true. Consequently, the former horn will be bracketed out in the ensuing chapters.

The chapter begins by investigating Marx's disparagement of various ethical standpoints, reaching the conclusion that he had consistently detested ethical analysis and criticism *tout court* (4.2). The subsequent section examines this "problem" from another angle. Its chief aim is to examine those passages in which his treatment of exploitation in capitalism appears to endorse a version of moral positivism. Yet, this position lends itself to the untenable conclusion—for which Marx himself was chiefly responsible—that he adopted the "bourgeois standpoint" in his assessment of capitalism (4.3).

Additional information is presented in 4.4 to further explain why this conclusion is untenable. More specifically, this section illustrates Marx's uncompromised opposition to, and support for the abolition of, both "direct slavery" and "veiled slavery" (wage-

---

[1] Throughout this work, I use the terms "moral" and "ethical" synonymously. Following Ruth Groff's wisdom, "My claim is that Marx has a view about what is good without qualification, and I am just as happy to call such a commitment a moral theory as I am to call it an ethics." Groff, "On the Ethical Contours of Thin Aristotelian Marxism," 314.

[2] For the complexity of these positions and definitions, paradoxes they entail, and very thoughtful attempts to resolve them, see Lukes, *Marxism and Morality*; Peffer, *Marxism, Morality, and Social Justice*. Other important accounts include Kamenka, *The Ethical Foundations of Marxism*; Brenkert, *Marx's Ethics of Freedom*; Kain, *Marx and Ethics*; Wilde, *Ethical Marxism and its Radical Critics*.

labor). This brief discussion will allow us to discern the most fundamental reason behind Marx's condemnation of capitalism. As 4.4 further reiterates, *inter alia*, Marx had very consistently condemned capitalism for perpetuating "slavery" (unfreedom), which is the core aspect of alienation. Without engaging in definition-mongering, the chapter concludes that the ethical nature of his condemnation of alienation is obvious.

4.2 Critique of Ethical Standpoints

In *The German Ideology*, Marx and Engels reproach Immanuel Kant's moral philosophy for being "purely ideological":

> The characteristic form which French liberalism, based on real class interests, assumed in Germany we find again in Kant. Neither he, nor the German middle class, whose whitewashing spokesman he was, noticed that these theoretical ideas of the bourgeoisie had as their basis material interests and a *will* that was conditioned and determined by the material relations of production. Kant, therefore …, made the materially motivated determinations of the will of the French bourgeois into *pure* self-determinations of "*free will*," of the will in and for itself, of the human will, and so converted it into purely ideological conceptual determinations and moral postulates.

Here, they appear to unfairly reduce Kant's moral doctrine to a mere cloak for the "shameless bourgeois profit-making." Since this passage does not generalize this verdict, it might—or not—be read simply as a critique of Kant's doctrine. One would even be apt to conclude that the reference to "bourgeois profit-making" as "shameless" itself implies a moral judgment. However, the authors state in the very same text that "the communists do not preach *morality* at all." This often-quoted passage is a reaction to Max Stirner, who apparently thinks "the communists do not oppose egoism to selflessness or selflessness to egoism." [3]

The anti-morality, individualist Stirner's charge against the communists seems to be that they are moral, for they wish to "do away with the 'private individual' for the sake of the 'general', selfless man." (This charge is still levelled against them today.)

---

[3] Marx and Engels, *The German Ideology*, 195, 247.

Consequently, they wish to sacrifice individual freedom at the altar of the common good.[4]

As we just saw, Marx and Engels flatly deny the charge of preaching morality. The communists, they go on to reiterate, "are very well aware that egoism, just as much as selflessness, is in definite circumstances a necessary form of the self-assertion of individuals." However, rather than preferring the one over the other, they "rather demonstrate" the "material source" of "the contradiction" between egoism and selflessness in modern society. As the reference to the *Deutsch–Französische Jahrbücher* indicates, they imply here that "On the Jewish Question" demonstrates the sense in which this is the case. By the same token—because this text focuses on alienation, this reference implies that the "material source" of the opposition between the private and the general individual is socio-economic alienation. Therefore, the central point here is that the "contradiction" will become irrelevant with the abolition of the "material" sources of alienation; preaching "to people the moral demand: love one another, do not be egoists, etc.," will not do. Such preaching is called "sentimental" and "ideological,"[5] and therefore ineffectual at best.

In short, Marx and Engels deny preaching morality in *The German Ideology*. Their critique of Kant supplements this denial with the troubling equation of all morality with the ideas that justify the interests of the ruling class. Proudhon is also disparaged for similar reasons in various texts, including the *Manifesto*.[6]

This has led to the claim that, in the *Manifesto*, Marx and Engels want to abolish all morality, as opposed to not preaching it themselves.[7] In the most directly relevant passage, they respond to the accusation that communists ignore "'eternal truths, such as

---

[4] For an insightful discussion of Marx's critique of Stirner in *The German Ideology*, see Thomas, "Karl Marx and Max Stirner," 159-79. For a very informative recent collection of essays, see ed. Newman, *Max Stirner*.

[5] Marx and Engels, *The German Ideology*, 247.

[6] Marx, "On Proudhon," 28-29; Marx, *The Poverty of Philosophy*, 167, 178. Marx and Engels, *Manifesto of the Communist Party*, 513.

[7] Marx clearly "accepts the charge that Communism ... abolishes ... all morality, instead of constituting [it] on a new basis." Miller, *Analyzing Marx*, 15. According to Kain, Marx accepted this only from 1845 to 1856. Kain, *Marx and Ethics*, 83. As I Illustrate below, this view is not accurate.

Freedom, Justice, etc., that are common to all states of society. But Communism abolishes eternal truths, it abolishes all religion and all morality, instead of constituting them on a new basis; it therefore acts in contradiction to all past historical experience.'"[8] Against these charges, the *Manifesto* polemically responds: "All property relations in the past have continually been subject to historical change consequent upon the change in historical conditions."[9] Therefore, the communistic aim to abolish the bourgeois form of private property cannot possibly be a violation of an allegedly eternal notion of justice or morality, since these are themselves "the outgrowth of the conditions of ... bourgeois production."[10]

Differently put, "The Communist revolution is the most radical rupture with traditional property relations; no wonder that its development involves the most radical rupture with traditional ideas."[11] Such ideas apparently include morality. If so, "the Communists" do not seek to abolish morality, etc., per se. Rather, they seek to abolish its material basis. This suggests, implausibly so, that "eternal ideas" will vanish in communism.

"The Communists," Marx and Engels go on to argue, derive their "theoretical conclusions" from "an actual class struggle ... going on under our very eyes," and declare unequivocally that "abolition of private property" is their ultimate aim. It turns out, they wish to abolish private property because it is based on the "exploitation of the many by the few," which bestows upon the few (capitalists) a dominant "social status," with which they "command" the labor of others. In the creation of this form of property, the worker sinks to the level of "bare existence." Otherwise put, the system of private property "does not promote the existence of the worker." It makes them "dependent" and suppresses their "individuality."[12]

To *us*, these criticisms of various forms of alienation have a moral purchase. Marx and Engels obviously disagree. They do so on the puzzling ground that only those ideas that attempt to harmonize the interests of classes, which amounts to perpetuating

---

[8] Marx and Engels, *Manifesto of the Communist Party*, 504.
[9] Ibid., 498.
[10] Ibid., 501.
[11] Ibid., 504.
[12] Ibid., 498-99.

the interests of the ruling class, count as moral. If so, they maintain, their own ideas regarding the abolition of private property and the emancipation of the worker cannot be dubbed "moral."

Marx remained evidently averse to framing his critique of alienation (broadly conceived) in ethical terms. For instance, he only regretfully included (to satisfy the other members) ethically charged terms in his program for the Working Men's International Association. "I was obliged to insert two sentences about 'DUTY and 'RIGHT", and ditto about "TRUTH, MORALITY AND JUSTICE' in the preamble to the rules, but these are so placed that they can do no harm," he explains to Engels in a private letter.[13]

Likewise, in the *Critique of the Gotha Program*, Marx describes this sort of "harm" (harm?) entailed in the demands of certain German socialists for "'equal right' and 'fair distribution'" as a "crime" against his own "realistic outlook," an attempt to replace it with such "obsolete verbal rubbish."[14] In a letter to one Friedrich Adolph Sorge, written two years later, he complains about this same tendency, in similar terms and for similar reasons.

> In Germany a corrupt spirit is asserting itself in our party ... The compromise with the Lassalleans has led to further compromise with other waverers; in Berlin (via Most) with Dühring and his "admirers", not to mention a whole swarm of immature undergraduates and over-wise graduates who want to give socialism a "higher, idealistic" orientation, i.e. substitute for the materialist basis (which calls for serious, objective study if one is to operate thereon) a modern mythology with its goddesses of Justice, Liberty, Equality and Fraternité.[15]

The visceral reaction of a revolutionary to the demands of "Justice, Liberty, Equality and Fraternité" appears odd to me. It is also strange that here, as elsewhere, Marx seems to assume that making such demands and engaging "in serious, objective study" to understand "the material basis" of socialism are mutually exclusive mental exercises. It is thus not surprising that he describes his own

---

[13] "Marx to Frederick Engels, November 4, 1864," 18.
[14] Marx, *Critique of the Gotha Program*, 87-88.
[15] "Marx to Friedrich Adolph Sorge, October 19, 1877," 283

doctrine as scientific in the way chemistry is in *Capital*, stressing that it has nothing to do with ethically-relevant assessments and demands, such as Proudhon's appeal to "*justice éternelle*" to "reform the actual production of commodities [which entail 'usury'], and the actual legal system corresponding thereto, in accordance with this idea." "What opinion should we have of a chemist," Marx asks sarcastically, "who, instead of studying the actual laws of the molecular changes in the composition and decomposition of matter … claimed to regulate the composition and decomposition of matter by means of the "eternal ideas", of '*naturalité*' and '*affinité*'?"[16]

As this ill-conceived analogy illustrates, Marx could be surprisingly thoughtless about certain issues, especially "eternal ideas." At any rate, this and the preceding examples illustrate his rejection of all appeals to ethics to either condemn or solve social problems. There appear to be some reasons to believe that his rejection is associated with a version of moral positivism.

4.3 Untenable Moral Positivism

According to Karl Popper, moral positivism holds that "there is no moral standard but the one which exists … The practical aspect of this theory is this. A moral criticism of the existing state of affairs is impossible, since this state itself determines the moral standard of things."[17] Several passages in Marx's writings justify the verdict that he was a moral positivist in this sense. One such passage reads:

> The circumstance, that on the one hand the daily sustenance of labor power costs only half a day's labor, while on the other hand the very same labor power can work during a whole day, that consequently the value which its use during one day creates, is double what he pays for that use, this circumstance is, without doubt, a piece of good luck for the buyer, but by no means an injury [*unrecht*] to the seller.[18]

---

[16] Marx, *Capital*, Vol. 1, 95-96.
[17] Popper, *The Open Society and Its Enemies: Hegel and Marx*, 227. According to Popper, Marx employed moral standards in his critique of capitalism. Ibid.
[18] Marx, *Capital*, Vol. 1, 204.

According to Eduard Bernstein, Marx contradicts himself when he simultaneously characterizes the value-exchange between the capitalist and the worker as exploitative, and so injurious (unjust) in this sense, and also as just.[19] Others, such as Robert C. Tucker and Allen W. Wood, however, claim that Marx does not contradict himself since he thinks the exchange is just (the so-called "Tucker-Wood thesis"). The passage just quoted serves as their primary piece of evidence to produce the following verdict on Marx's behalf, and this in Wood's wording: "The appropriation of surplus value by capital, therefore, involves no unequal or unjust exchange."[20]

A portion of this verdict is flatly false: The claim that, in Marx's view, no "unequal" exchange occurs in the appropriation of "surplus" value is an oxymoron. More specifically, the passage under our scrutiny clearly depicts an unequal exchange. Yet, to say that the exchange in question is unequal is not to say that it is therefore unjust. There is a sense in which Marx thought this *unequal* exchange is just, however.

As Ziyad I. Husami aptly points out, the passage in question "occurs in a context in which Marx is plainly satirizing capitalism. Marx, immediately after the passage in question, characterizes the appropriation of surplus labor as a 'trick.'"[21] In other words, about two pages earlier, Marx tells us that he here considers the viewpoint of "our capitalist who is at home in his vulgar economy."[22] If so, the famous passage expresses the view of "our capitalist," who "foresaw this state of things, and that was the cause of his laughter." What unfolds in this context is consistent with a strategy Marx often utilizes; it involves unmasking and inverting the assumptions of his opponents. Here, the unmasking comes in the form of a demonstration of how the value of the product is "greater than the value advanced for its production." Consequently, "a surplus value ... has been created," which is precisely the unpaid value created by the worker and appropriated by the capitalist without an equivalent.[23]

---

[19] Bernstein, *Selected Writings, 1900–1921*, 91.
[20] Wood, "The Marxian Critique of Justice," 263. Also see Tucker, *Philosophy and Myth in Karl Marx*, 18-19.
[21] Husami, "Marx on Distributive Justice," 30.
[22] Marx, *Capital,* Vol. 1, 202.
[23] Ibid., 204.

Again, Marx's conclusion does not imply that the appropriation of the surplus value constitutes injustice. Indeed, he thinks it is just in a specific sense. We encounter this sense in his reaction to Adolph Wagner's interpretation of his work. The "obscurantist," says Marx,

> falsely attributes to me [the view] that "the *surplus value* produced by the laborers *alone* was left to the capitalists in an unwarranted [or improper (*ungebührlicher*)] manner." Well, I say the direct opposite, namely, that commodity production is necessarily, at a certain point, turned into "capitalistic" commodity production, and that according to the *law of value* governing it, "surplus value" is properly due to the capitalist and not to the laborer.[24]

What Marx means to say here is further clarified in another passage: "I demonstrate in detail that ... the capitalist—as soon as he pays the worker the real value of his labor-power [which is the cost of reproducing and maintaining it]—would have every right, i.e. such right as corresponds to this mode of production, to *surplus-value*." "But," Marx adds, "all this does not make 'profit on capital' the '*constitutive*' *element* of value but only proves that the value not '*constituted*' by the labor of capitalist conceals a portion which he can appropriate 'legally,' i.e. without infringing the law corresponding to the exchange of commodities."[25] In this context, Marx also says the capitalist "robs" the worker but claims that this is consistent with his right.

On the one hand, Marx might be read as offering an uninstructive position in these passages, basically claiming that the exploitation of the worker in capitalism is legal, and so just in this sense. However, he also appears to equate the law or right with ethicality, which then lends itself to the conclusion that whatever is legal is also proper, and so just in this sense also, and that these issues are objectively settled by the mode of production that gives rise to them. But, objects G. A. Cohen, to rob anyone, in this case the worker, "is to commit an injustice, and a system which is 'based on theft' [Marx] is based on injustice." Therefore, Marx "did not

---

[24] Marx, "Marginal Notes on Adolph Wagner's *Lehrbuch der politischen Oekonomie*," 558.
[25] Ibid., 535-36.

believe that capitalism was unjust, because he was confused about justice."[26]

Be this as it may, the general picture remains unaltered. As Wood further points out, even though Marx had consistently maintained that "capitalist exploitation alienates, dehumanizes and degrades wage laborers," he nevertheless thought "there is nothing about it which is wrongful or unjust." Once again, his assumption here is that Marx thought all "matters involving rights or justice [or morality]" in capitalism are reducible to its own material standpoint.[27] In short, "there is no sign that Marx sees anything morally wrong or unjust about ... capitalism."[28] It is thus apt to characterize him as an "'amoralist,' even 'immoralist,'"[29] or a moral positivist.

Wood's interpretation entails far-reaching ramifications. As Husami points out, it implies that Marx adopted "the standpoint of the ruling class" in "his evaluation of capitalism." If this were the case, he "would have abandoned his critical-revolutionary standpoint."[30] The problem with Husami's approach is that he mainly blames the likes of Wood for this dilemma, glossing over Marx's contribution to it.

We now arrive at a paradox: Marx adopts both the bourgeois standpoint (which justifies the existing state of affairs) and the critical-revolutionary one (which seeks to abolish them). The problem at hand is revealed vividly in Marx's following comment: A "content is just whenever it corresponds, is appropriate, to the mode of production. It is unjust whenever it contradicts that mode. Slavery on the basis of capitalist production is unjust ..."[31] Curiously, he does not say, on the basis of another form of production, slavery is just, even though what he says here implies this conclusion. He also does not say, on the basis of capitalist production, wage-slavery is just, even though this too is implied. However, as we are about to see, he consistently condemned both forms of slavery. This means that he thought condemning them and

---

[26] Cohen, "Review of Wood's *Karl Marx*," 443-44.
[27] Wood, *Karl Marx*, 43.
[28] Ibid., 153.
[29] Ibid., 151.
[30] Husami, "Marx on Distributive Justice," 62-63.
[31] Marx, *Capital,* Vol. 3, 337-38.

referring to them as "unjust" are different things, and that by calling them "just," he neither approves them nor remains indifferent toward them.

4.4 Ethical Condemnation of Slavery

In a letter to Sigfrid Meyer, Marx explains how his severe illness forced him to devote all his dwindling energies to completing the first volume of *Capital*, which meant not only delaying his reply to Meyer but also sacrificing his "health, happiness, and family." With a not-so-veiled link to the ultimate aim of his *magnum opus*, he then remarks: "If one wanted to be an ox, one could, of course, turn one's back on the sufferings of humanity and look after one's own hide."[32] Evidently, in addition to the personal and familial ones, many other types of "sufferings" concerned Marx. The ones that he frequently highlighted are subsumed under the concept of alienation (see Chapter 2). This section focuses on his condemnation of "wage-slavery" in capitalism, which unfreedom I regard as foundational to his theory of alienation.

Marx had consistently condemned all forms of slavery. For instance, he was concerned with "direct slavery" far more than it is usually supposed. In fact, he was one of the first to suggest a causal link between "direct slavery," colonialism, and the development of capitalism. We find this link in his *The Poverty of Philosophy*.[33] It is also present in *Capital*, where condemning descriptions of the "barbarities" entailed in the "primitive capital accumulation" abound. By extension, the link also creates a direct relationship between "the veiled slavery of the wage-earners in Europe" and "slavery pure and simple in the New World."[34] Many more similar links between slavery and the development of capitalism, the system of "veiled slavery," can be found in Marx's writings.[35]

One can also find in them one of the earliest criticisms of the white American workers for allowing "slavery to defile their own republic" together with "an oligarchy of 300,000 slaveholders." This is what Marx's January 1865 letter to Abraham Lincoln,

---

[32] "Marx to Meyer, April 30, 1867," 366.
[33] Marx, *The Poverty of Philosophy*, 167.
[34] Marx, *Capital*, Vol. 1, 739, 747.
[35] For a brief but effective compilation and analysis of such examples, see Lawrence, *Marx on American Slavery*.

written on behalf of the International Workingmen's Association, states. Tellingly, the irony in all this is not lost upon Marx, who notes how while "the Negro" was "mastered and sold without his concurrence," the "white-skinned laborer ... boasted ... [his] highest prerogative to sell himself and choose his own master."[36]

Otherwise put, as he puts it in *Capital*, the two slaveries are connected: "Labor cannot emancipate itself in the white skin where in the black it is branded. But out of the death of slavery a new life at once arose [in the United States]. The first fruit of the Civil War was the eight hours' agitation," a right step in direction of the emancipation of the working class (black and white).[37]

"In actual history (of [primitive] capital accumulation)," Marx also argues, "it is notorious that conquest, enslavement, robbery, murder, briefly, force play the great part."[38] This situation has normalized in developed capitalism. "To accumulate [capital] is to conquer the world of social wealth, to increase the mass of human beings exploited by him, and thus to extend both the direct and the indirect sway of the capitalist ... They [capitalists] enrich themselves chiefly by robbing.[39] "Along with the constantly diminishing number of the magnates of capital, who usurp and monopolize all advantages ..., grows the misery, oppression, slavery, degradation, exploitation" of the worker.[40] Marx arrives at a parallel conclusion in the third volume of *Capital*: "capital obtains

---

[36] Marx, "Address of the International Workingmen's Association to Abraham," 19-21. Marx's letter was occasioned by Lincoln's reelection. It also clearly expresses Marx's ongoing support for the abolition of slavery. Moreover, some of Marx's friends "had played an important role in winning the German émigré working class to the Republican cause." Nimtz, *Marx and Engels*, 170. One of his and Engels' close friends, Joseph Weydemeyer ("the first American Marxist") even fought against the forces of slavery under Lincoln's command. Obermann, *Joseph Weydemeyer*. Blackburn assumes that Lincoln himself was familiar with Marx's journalistic writings. Blackburn, *Marx and Lincoln*. What we know for certain is that he received Marx's letter and, via the U.S. Ambassador in London, thanked him and his colleagues, "the friends of humanity," for their support for the common cause of emancipation.
[37] Marx, *Capital*, Vol. 1, 305.
[38] Ibid., 705.
[39] Ibid., 588–90.
[40] Ibid., 750.

this surplus-labor without an equivalent, and in essence always remains forced labor—no matter how much it may seem to result from free contractual agreement."[41]

Such comments as these clarify that Marx's condemnation of capitalism is not centered on such issues as simple exploitation (the appropriation of surplus value) and low-income. For instance, against the argument that rapid capital accumulation must be supported because it improves the material condition of the working class, he retorts that the rapid accumulation of capital means increasing the domination of capital ("hostile forces") over the worker. Thus, increased wages do not solve the problem Marx repeatedly calls a form of "slavery." He drives this very point home in "Wage Labor and Capital":

> To say that the most favorable condition for wage labor is the most rapid possible growth of productive capital is only to say that the more rapidly the working class increases and enlarges the power that is hostile to it, the wealth that does not belong to it and that rules over it, the more favorable will be the conditions under which it is allowed to labor anew at increasing bourgeois wealth, at enlarging the power of capital, content with forging for itself the golden chains by which the bourgeoisie drags it in its train.[42]

Marx plays the same tune in his *Critique of the Gotha Program*: "the system of wage labor is a system of slavery, and indeed of a slavery which becomes more severe in proportion as the social productive forces of labor develop, whether the worker receives better or worse payment." If so, to say that capitalism should be abolished because it cannot provide more than a low-maximum in wages, as the Lassalleans argue, is tantamount to saying, "Slavery must be abolished because the feeding of slaves in the system of slavery cannot exceed a low maximum."[43] Let us not forget the *Manuscripts of 1844*: "An enforced *increase of wages* ... would therefore be nothing but *better payment for the slave,* and would not win for the worker or for labor their human status and dignity."[44]

---

[41] Marx, *Capital*, Vol. 3, 806.
[42] Marx, "Wage Labor and Capital," 221
[43] Marx, *Critique of the Gotha Program,* 92.
[44] Karl Marx, *Economic and Philosophic Manuscripts of 1844*, 280.

My emphasis on its cruciality should not be read as an argument to the effect that Marx ultimately reduces the problem of alienation to that "slavery." Still, even when he considers alienation in a wholesale manner, he often emphasizes this very problem. This, I believe, is evident in the following, powerful passage, found in *Capital*:

> Within the capitalist system all methods for raising the social productiveness of labor are brought about at the cost of the individual laborer; all means for the development of production transform themselves into means of domination over, and exploitation of, the producers; they mutilate the laborer into a fragment of a man, degrade him to the level of an appendage of a machine, destroy every remnant of charm in his work and turn it into a hated toil; they estrange from him the intellectual potentialities of the labor process in the same proportion as science is incorporated in it as an independent power; they distort the conditions under which he works, subject him during the labor process to a despotism the more hateful for its meanness; they transform his life-time into working-time, and drag his wife and child beneath the wheels of the Juggernaut of capital. But all methods for the production of surplus value are at the same time methods of accumulation; and every extension of accumulation becomes again a means for the development of those methods. It follows therefore that in proportion as capital accumulates, the lot of the laborer, be his payment high or low, must grow worse. The law, finally, that always equilibrates the relative surplus population, or industrial reserve army, to the extent and energy of accumulation, this law rivets the laborer to capital more firmly than the wedges of Vulcan did Prometheus to the rock. It establishes an accumulation of misery, corresponding with accumulation of capital. Accumulation of wealth at one pole is, therefore, at the same time accumulation of misery, agony of toil, slavery, ignorance, brutality, mental degradation, at the opposite pole, *i.e.,* on the side of the class that produces its own product in the form of capital.[45]

---

[45] Karl Marx, *Capital*, Vol. 1, 639–40.

Marx's portrayal of the multifaceted impoverishment (alienation) of the working class here obviously entails value-ridden judgements about what he takes to be essential facts about capitalism. Indeed, he refers to such facts as "modern evils" in the preface to the first German edition of the same *Capital*.[46] Surely, his assessment of them is not at all based on the "bourgeois" standpoint; nor are his various characterization of such "evils" the conclusions of a "chemist" or an "empiricist" of socio-economic relations, merely juggling "dead facts."[47]

***

Although Marx's thoughts in the lengthy quote from *Capital* generally speak for themselves, three observations about them are in order. First, the critical thoughts he expresses in them assume the theory of alienation, explicated in Chapter 2, meaning that they condemn various forms of alienation. Second, it is difficult to ignore his potent humanism, which underpins these critical thoughts, regardless of whether one, or Marx himself, prefers to call them "ethical" or something else. I call them "ethical" because they are.[48]

More importantly, the use of the term "ethical" helps us clarify that his analysis of capitalism cannot be reduced to "scientific" articulation of its technical problems or, as some would have it, to a mere statement of facts. This brings us to the third observation. After reading such comments as the lengthy one just quoted, it makes little sense to agree with the claim that the "materialist" Marx was

---

[46] Ibid., 9.

[47] Elsewhere, Marx and Engels depict their science as "the study of the actual life-process and the activity of individuals of each epoch," adding that "As soon as this active life-process is described, history ceases to be a collection of dead facts as it is with the empiricists (themselves still abstract), or an imagined activity of imagined subjects, as with the idealists." Marx and Engels, *The German Ideology*, 37.

[48] According to Wood, Marx has a "recognizably Aristotelian conception of human self-actualization, the development and exercise of our 'human essential powers'." However, he claims that this does not justify attributing to Marx a moral foundation. Wood, *Karl Marx*, 128. For an excellent critique of Wood and others in this regard, see Groff, "On the Ethical Contours of Thin Aristotelian Marxism." For a rich discussion on this issue, see ed. George E. McCarthy, *Marx and Aristotle*. Also see McCarthy, *Marx and Social Justice*.

"scientifically" indifferent to human suffering or slavery entailed in alienation.

The question now becomes whether the "ethical" ground of his critique of alienation is related to his justification of revolution. While the relationship may appear obvious, there are important reasons to doubt it. These reasons are generally related to Marx's economic-determinist commitment to the idea that the communist revolution is both inevitable and has nothing to do with political agency and ethical judgement. The next chapter attempts to explain how Marx was not very consistent in this regard either and, in the final analysis, his defense of revolution is (also) "ethically" grounded.

Necessities of Revolution

5.1 Introduction

Many scholars deny that Marx deemed the future communist revolution inevitable, while others—some approvingly and some disapprovingly—defend the contrary view. As 5.2 illustrates, the inevitability claim occurs frequently in Marx's writings. It is often attached to the rigidly historical-materialist claim that revolutions ultimately occur independently of political will. Like many others who have thought about this issue, I regard the claim as very problematic at best. However, my main aim in this section is to record its various versions, as well as its repeated presence, in Marx various writings.

Acknowledging this fact seems necessary before proceeding to show how he had also repeatedly defended certain views that appear to oppose the agentless inevitability claim in various ways. Three types of such views are considered in 5.3: (1) Marx's castigation of those socialists who opposed political struggles to improve the condition of the working class; (2) his insistence that communism cannot be realized without a political revolution; (3) his denunciation of those who remained indifferent toward the abject condition of the working class. In these contexts, the claim of inevitability is questioned by Marx himself from various angles.

If not historically-materially inevitable, if it must be willfully *made*, then the question now becomes why revolution ought to be made in the first place. This question is closely related to the issue of communist-revolutionary consciousness and conscience. What is its ground? After reviewing the available evidence on this issue, 5.4 concludes that such consciousness, according to Marx, ultimately arises from the contemplation of the alienated-dehumanized condition of the working class. This gives Marx's defense of revolution an ethical foundation, leading to the conclusion that capitalism must be overthrown because it fetters human freedom and well-being—or, which is the same thing, perpetuates all-around alienation. This conclusion, it goes without saying, dovetails the conclusion of the previous chapter. It also anticipates the conclusions of the subsequent ones.

5.2 Historical Necessity and Inevitability of Revolution

On many occasions, Marx derives the inevitability claim from a theory that many dub "historical materialism." An early statement of a version of this theory appears in *The German Ideology*: The "contradiction between the productive forces and the form of intercourse [the existing social relations] ... necessarily ... bursts out in a revolution." This claim is generalized for all historical epochs when Marx and Engels insist that "all [social and ideological] collisions in history have their origin, according to our view, in the contradiction between the productive forces and the form of [social] intercourse."[1] The authors use the same view to predict the impeding communist revolution as well.[2] Obviously, the boisterous claim about said "contradiction" being the "origin" of "all collisions" smacks of unacceptable reductionism. Among other things, it rejects, especially, the "illusions" of the revolutionaries who stress the importance of "their own activity" in making these revolutions.[3]

The same historical-materialist theory is utilized to explain the "bourgeois" revolution in the *Manifesto*:

> We see then: the means of production and of exchange, on whose foundation the bourgeoisie built itself up, were generated in feudal society. At a certain stage in the development of these means of production and of exchange, the conditions under which feudal society produced and exchanged, the feudal organization of agriculture and manufacturing industry, in one word, the feudal relations of property became no longer compatible with the already developed productive forces; they became so many fetters. They had to be burst asunder; they were burst asunder.[4]

In a nutshell, Marx and Engels maintain here that revolutions occur when the existing "relations of property" *fetter* the development of "productive forces." Although the two main categories of this formula are ambiguous enough to make one

---

[1] Marx and Engels, *The German Ideology*, 74-75.
[2] Ibid., 52.
[3] Ibid., 74.
[4] Marx and Engels, *Manifesto of the Communist Party*, 489.

wonder what all this means, it is relatively clear that the development of the forces of production is often given causal primacy. G. A. Cohen has assembled numerous passages from Marx's various works to make a convincing case for "the primacy thesis,"[5] which some call "technological determinism." It is also possible to find, as many critics of Cohen's argument have, other theories of revolution in Marx's writings, such as the one that emphasizes class struggles, not to forget the related theories of economic crisis, overproduction, and the law or tendency of the rate of profit to fall. In short, Marx's writings do not yield a coherent answer in this regard.

However, Marx and Engels do rely on the fetters-theory, based on the primacy thesis, to predict the allegedly impending communist revolution in the *Manifesto* also: "The productive forces at the disposal of society no longer tend to further the development of the relations of bourgeois property; on the contrary, they have become too powerful for these relations by which they are fettered." It is thus just a matter of time before the "weapons" (productive forces) the "bourgeoisie forged" against feudalism "bring death to itself."[6]

According to Marx and Engels, furthermore, in preparing the conditions of its development "the bourgeoise has also called into existence" its own executioners, namely, "the modern working class—the proletarians," the other "weapons" and "productive force" of its foretold impeding demise.

> The advance of industry, whose involuntary promoter is the bourgeoisie, replaces the isolation of the laborers, due to competition, by their revolutionary combination, due to association. The development of Modern Industry, therefore, cuts from under its feet the very foundation on which the bourgeoisie produces and appropriates products. What the bourgeoisie, therefore, produces, above all, is its own gravediggers. Its fall and the victory of the proletariat are equally inevitable [*unvermeidlich*].[7]

The link between the fetters-theory of revolution and the prediction of the proletarian revolution in this passage is not clear to

---

[5] Cohen, *Karl Marx's Theory of History*, Ch. 6 and throughout.
[6] Marx and Engels, *Manifesto of the Communist Party*, 490.
[7] Ibid., 496.

me. Be that as it may, Marx and Engels obviously assert here that the proletarian-communist revolution is inevitable, and this will be ultimately settled by material-economic forces, not the human will, that the latter will come into play—in the form of acute class struggles—as a consequence of the development of such forces.

The inevitability claim is also repeated in one of Marx's letters to Joseph Weydemeyer. In it, he claims to be the first to have shown, *inter alia*, that "the class struggle [in bourgeois society] necessarily leads to the *dictatorship of the proletariat*," and then necessarily "to the *abolition of all classes* and to a *classless society*."[8] Whether the class struggle in question depends on the fetters-theory is not here explained. In any case, to say that class struggle will necessarily lead to the abolition of capitalism is to rob the actors involved in this struggle of their agency.

The fetters-theory of revolution reappears, together with the inevitability claim, in Marx's famous "Preface" to *A Contribution to the Critique of Political Economy*:

> At a certain stage of development, the material productive forces of society come into conflict with the existing relations of production or—this merely expresses the same thing in legal terms—with the property relations within the framework of which they have operated hitherto. From forms of development of the productive forces these relations turn into their fetters. Then begins an era of social revolution. The changes in the economic foundation lead sooner or later to the transformation of the whole immense [political] superstructure.[9]

Once more, the fetters-theory renders the human will quite secondary, if not utterly insignificant: "In the social production of their existence, men inevitably enter into definite relations, which are independent of their will, namely relations of production appropriate to a given stage in the development of their material forces of production."[10] If so, the new society will likewise emerge quite independently of human will. It will do so inevitably, "sooner or later."

Elsewhere, Marx disparages the "ignorant louts such as

---

[8] "Marx to Joseph Weydemeyer, March 5, 1852," 62.
[9] Marx, *A Contribution to the Critique of Political Economy,* 263.
[10] Ibid.

Heinzen" for regarding "the social conditions in which the bourgeoisie is dominant as the final product, the *non plus ultra* [the highest point] of history," and so for failing to see the "transient necessity of the bourgeois regime itself."[11] This claim calls to mind our next, more crucial example: Marx's description of his dialectic in the "Afterword" (1873) to the second German edition of *Capital*:

> In its rational form, [dialectic] is a scandal and abomination to bourgeoisdom and its doctrinaire professors, because it includes in its comprehension and affirmative recognition of the existing state of things, at the same time also, the recognition of the negation of that state, of its inevitable breaking up; because it regards every historically developed social form as in fluid movement, and therefore takes into account its transient nature not less than its momentary existence; because it lets nothing impose upon it, and is in its essence critical and revolutionary.[12]

Marx's comment is occasioned by a review of *Capital*, in which, as far as Marx is concerned, the Russian reviewer "generously" describes his dialectic method:

> "Marx only troubles himself about one thing: to show, by rigid scientific investigation, the necessity of successive determinate orders of social conditions, and to establish, as impartially as possible, the facts that serve him for fundamental starting-points. For this it is quite enough, if he proves, at the same time, both the necessity of the present order of things, and the necessity of another order into which the first must inevitably pass over; and this all the same, whether men believe or do not believe it, whether they are conscious or unconscious of it. Marx treats the social movement as a process of natural history, governed by laws."[13]

To reiterate, the "rigid scientific investigation," which Marx refers to as his dialectic, predicts the inevitable transition of capitalism into communism, and this "whether men believe or do not believe it, whether they are conscious or unconscious of it." The

---

[11] "Marx to Joseph Weydemeyer, March 5, 1852," 62.

[12] Marx, *Capital*, Vol. 1, 20.

[13] Ibid., 18.

reviewer surely took his cue from Marx, who declares in the "Preface" to the first German edition of *Capital* that "the ultimate aim of this work [is] to lay bare the economic law of motion of modern society."[14] The very lengthy articulation of this law in this work eventually leads Marx to the conclusion that "capitalist production begets, with the inexorability of a law of Nature, its own negation. It is the negation of negation." The second negation is the anticipated arrival of communism, based on "the possession in common of the land and of the means of production."[15] That he thinks the second negation is inevitable is reiterated in a footnote Marx appends to this very discussion. The footnote quotes the famous passage form the *Manifesto*: "What the bourgeoisie, therefore, produces, above all, is its own gravediggers. Its fall and the victory of the proletariat are equally inevitable."[16]

Basically, regardless of the specific theory or claim endorsing it, the inevitability claim is inherent in one of Marx's most basic assumptions about capitalism, viz., it is necessarily "transient," which implies that its transcendence is inevitable. As Johann Most—using Marx's own corrections and suggestions—puts it in the second edition of his *Kapital und Arbeit*, written to popularize *Capital*, Marx (allegedly) accomplishes two seemingly opposites goals in *Capital*. On the one hand, he "destroys all optimistic illusions" by proving that "no society can be conceived and made according to individual plans." On the other hand, he instills the socialists with "the fullest confidence in the victory" of revolution by proving that "capitalism contains the seeds of socialism and communism, and that the former," in accordance with its "own laws" of motion, resembling the "necessity of the laws of nature," "must evolve into the latter."[17] In short, "the capitalist mode of production is actually only a transitional form, which must lead through its own organism to a higher, to a co-operative mode of production, to socialism."[18] Most would eventually become an anarchist-voluntarist (see Chapter 7),

---

[14] Ibid., 10.
[15] Ibid., 751.
[16] Ibid., 751 n.1.
[17] Most, *Kapital und Arbeit*, 4. For evidence of Marx's heavy-handed involvement, see "Marx to Friedrich Adolph Sorge, June 14, 1876," 125.
[18] Most, *Kapital und Arbeit*, 59.

5.3 Beyond Inevitability

The preceding section illustrates Marx's lifelong confidence in the inevitability of communist revolution. Yet, many of his writings, including the ones in which the inevitability-assumption is defended, urge one to conclude that his confidence in "the economic law of motion of modern society" had its limits. Such passages may be thematically divided into three distinctive types. First, Marx was consistently hostile to those who either refrained from or opposed political struggles to improve the condition of the working class and to achieve socialism. The other side of this coin, and second, is his insistence that revolution must be a deliberate, political act, without which the arrival of socialism would be jeopardized, if not rendered impossible. Third, he had consistently denounced those who remained indifferent toward "human suffering," which implies that its eradication is an ethical imperative for all.

An elaborate version of the first type is found in the *Manifesto*. Some pages after declaring the inevitability of the proletarian revolution, this text turns into a disparaging critique of various socialist traditions. The German or "true" socialism is called to task for "proclaiming its supreme and impartial contempt of all class struggles." The conservative or bourgeois socialism of the likes of Proudhon is disparaged for desiring to preserve "all the advantages of modern social conditions without the struggles and dangers necessarily resulting therefrom," and requiring "that the proletariat should ... cast away all its hateful ideas concerning the bourgeoisie." "A second ... form of this Socialism sought to depreciate every revolutionary movement in the eyes of the working class," failing to see the necessity of the "abolition of the bourgeois relations of production, an abolition that can be affected only by a revolution." Various utopians, such as Henri de Saint-Simon, Charles Fourier, Étienne Cabet, and Robert Owen, are also criticized for rejecting "all revolutionary action." The followers of these original utopians also "endeavor... to deaden the class struggle and to reconcile the class antagonisms." In short, they "violently oppose all political action on the part of the working class."[19]

Contrary to these traditions, "the Communists never cease, for a single instant, to instill into the working class the clearest possible

---

[19] Marx and Engels, *Manifesto of the Communist Party*, 513-17.

recognition of the hostile antagonism between bourgeoisie and proletariat ... They openly declare that their ends can be attained only by the forcible overthrow of all existing social conditions."[20] Marx and Engels make a similar claim in *The German Ideology*: "Revolution is necessary ... because the *ruling* class cannot be overthrown in any other way."[21] The same conviction is also expressed in an 1844 work: "*socialism* cannot be realized without [political] *revolution*."[22]

Of course, these claims do not necessarily contradict the claim that a revolution is inevitable. To wit, one could cogently argue that the realization of socialism is inevitable, and that revolution is necessarily the political means with which it will come about.[23] However, the passages considered in this section imply that revolution must be deliberately made; otherwise it may not happen. At least on one occasion, that is, in his last public speech (1872), Marx defends the least ambivalent version of this view: "One day the worker will have to seize political supremacy to establish the new organization of labor; he will have to overthrow the old policy which supports the old institutions if he wants to escape the fate of the early Christians who, neglecting and despising politics, never saw their kingdom on earth."[24]

Another type of evidence also raises questions about Marx's commitment to the inevitability claim: He had consistently scorned those who remained indifferent to the sufferings of the working class, not to mention justifying them. For instance, his *The Poverty of Philosophy* contains an interesting critique of various "*fatalist* economists." These economists are divided into "Classics and Romantics." "In their theory," they are all as "indifferent ... as the bourgeois themselves are in practice to the sufferings of the proletarians who help them to acquire wealth." "The Classics, like

---

[20] Ibid., 519.

[21] Marx and Engels, *The German Ideology*, 52-53.

[22] Marx, "Critical Marginal Notes on the Article 'The King of Prussia and Social Reform' by a Prussian," 206.

[23] Or, as Cohen puts it, "I take it that something ... can also be inevitable because it is bound to happen not no matter what people do, but because of what people are bound, predictably, to do." Cohen, "Historical Inevitability and Human Agency in Marxism," 68.

[24] Marx, "On the Hague Congress," 255.

Adam Smith and Ricardo ..., have no other mission than that of showing how wealth is acquired in bourgeois production relations" and how these relations are "superior" to those of "feudal society." Poverty is in their eyes merely the pang which accompanies every childbirth, in nature as in industry." "The Romantics belong to our own age, in which ... poverty is engendered in as great abundance as wealth. The economists now pose as blasé fatalists, who, from their elevated position, cast a proudly disdainful glance at the human machines who manufacture wealth."[25]

The reference to workers as "human machines who manufacture wealth" obviously dovetails Marx's critical stance on alienation. Those who remain indifferent to it are condemnable, in his view. This also implies that, in his view, it matters a great deal whether one remains indifferent to human suffering or acts to eliminate it. Relatedly, in the letter to Weydemeyer, in which he claims to have discovered the inevitability of the dictatorship of the proletariat, he disparages Heinzen and the like for regarding the bourgeois society as the final and the highest point possible in history. This implies to him that they justify this society, and so ultimately act as "the servants of the bourgeoisie." This "servitude" is "revolting."[26]

For related reasons, despite "openly" avowing himself "the pupil of that mighty thinker," Marx was equally repulsed by Hegel and his followers. Thus, after the description of the "revolutionary" character of his dialectic in *Capital*, considered in the previous section, he juxtaposes it with the "mystified form" of Hegel's dialectic. This dialectic, he adds disparagingly, "became the fashion in Germany, because it seemed to transfigure and to glorify the existing state of things."[27]

The social Darwinists of his time receive a related disparagement from Marx. In his December 19, 1860, letter to

---

[25] Marx, *The Poverty of Philosophy*, 176-78.
[26] "Marx to Joseph Weydemeyer, March 5, 1852," 62. This is the same Heinzen who had caused some stir by attacking the communists, especially Engels, a few years earlier. Engels responded in kind with two articles, both published in October 1847. Marx had also taken his own swipes at Heinzen in the same journal with two articles. See Engels, "The Communists and Karl Heinzen"; Marx, "Moralizing Criticism and Critical Morality.
[27] Marx, *Capital*, Vol. 1, 18.

Engels, he writes: "*Natural Selection* ..., in the field of natural history, provides the basis of our views," despite its "crude English" method of development.[28] However, in another letter to Engels, written on June 18, 1862, he says: "It is remarkable how Darwin rediscovers, among the beasts and plants, the society of England with its division of labor, competition, opening up of new markets, 'inventions' and Malthusian 'struggle for existence.' It is Hobbes' *bellum omnium contra omnes* ...; in Darwin, the animal kingdom figures as civil society."[29] In a letter to Laura and Paul Lafargue (Marx's daughter and son-in-law), written in 1869, Marx repeats these lines almost verbatim, and then goes on to find in social Darwinism the perverse application of the natural-selection theory: "Darwinism conversely considers this [i.e., the presumed law of *bellum omnium contra omnes*] a conclusive reason for human society never to emancipate itself from its bestiality."[30] The ethical register of all this is difficult to overlook.[31] Also, "*bellum omnium contra omnes*" is but just another expression for social alienation.[32]

Clearly, while persistently holding on to the inevitability claim, Marx never yielded to any version of indifferentism, not to mention any view that appeared to justify, directly or indirectly, "the existing state of things." As we have seen all along, anyone who had made short work of "the sufferings of the proletarians" or "the sufferings of humanity" met with his ire. In this regard, and to requote, Marx has this to say in his letter of April 30, 1867 to Weydemeyer: "If one wanted to be an ox, one could, of course, turn one's back on the sufferings of humanity and look after one's own hide."[33] This

---

[28] "Marx to Frederick Engels, December 19, 1860," 232. For similar thoughts, see "Marx to Ferdinand Lassalle, January 16, 1861," 246.

[29] "Marx to Frederick Engels, June 18, 1862," 381.

[30] "Marx to Laura and Paul Lafargue, February 15, 1869," 217.

[31] Unlike Marx, Karl Kautsky attempted to provide a Darwinian-naturalist ethical basis for Marxism in his *Ethics and the Materialist Conception of History*. Evidently, reconciling Darwin with socialism was a widespread fad at the time. This phenomenon disturbed the Italian Marxist Antonio Labriola: "*Darwinism, political and social* ... has, like an epidemic, for many years invaded the mind of more than one thinker, and many more of the advocates and declaimers of sociology." Cited in Plekhanov, *Fundamental Problems of Marxism*, 112.

[32] See "On the Jewish Question," 155.

[33] "Marx to Sigfrid Meyer, April 30, 1867," 366.

statement implies an ethical obligation to do something about "the sufferings of humanity," to ultimately help bring about communism, in which avoidable human suffering would be eliminated. Donald C. Lee categorizes aptly the three kinds of necessity one encounters in Marx's works: "(1) historical inevitability [or necessity], (2) the hypothetical imperative, and (3) the categorical (moral) imperative." The first refers to the sort of inevitability we encountered in 4.2. The second refers to the one retrieved in this section. The third denotes moral necessity: "one ought to pursue the revolution because it is morally obligatory to establish a new society and revolution is morally the best or only way to achieve that end."[34] This latter meaning is retrieved from his various works in the next section.

5.4 The Ethical Ground of Revolutionary Consciousness

As this section illustrates, *mutatis mutandis*, said categorical obligation is the ground of what Marx calls "communist consciousness," which is really an ethical conscience. Before we explore this issue, let us first establish how he thought disseminating such consciousness (or "theory") is necessary to set in motion a mass revolutionary movement.

For instance, in his "Contribution to the Critique of Hegel's Philosophy of Right: Introduction," Marx famously states that "The weapon of criticism cannot, of course, replace criticism by weapons, material force must be overthrown by material force; but theory also becomes a material force as soon as it has gripped the masses."[35] Here, contrary to the widespread notion, urged by some of Marx's own vulgarly deterministic comments, ideas appear to be much more than mere epiphenomenal byproducts of things material.

Indeed, Marx and Engels declare in the *Manifesto* that spreading revolutionary ideas "to the great mass of the proletariat" is their mission, not least because they are "theoretically" more advanced than the proletariat.[36] Marx makes a similar argument elsewhere, claiming that "Where the working class is not yet far enough advanced" it must "be trained ... by continual agitation against and

---

[34] Lee, "The Concept of 'Necessity': Marx and Marcuse," 52, 47.
[35] Marx, "Contribution to the Critique of Hegel's Philosophy of Right: Introduction," 182.
[36] Marx and Engels, *Manifesto of the Communist Party*, 497-98.

a hostile attitude towards the policy of the ruling classes. Otherwise it will remain a plaything in their hands.[37]

One can find many more such passages in which Marx issues advise to workers. Alongside this practical Marx, we find the more philosophical Marx. A revolutionary theory has to demonstrate "*ad hominem*, and it demonstrates *ad hominem* as soon as it becomes radical," writes the latter Marx, adding that "to be radical is to grasp the root of the matter. But for man the root is man himself." On the one hand, this is consistent with "the teaching that man is the highest being for man." On the other hand, it leads to "the *categorical imperative to overthrow all relations* in which man is debased, enslaved, forsaken, despicable being."[38]

Marx goes on to argue that this imperative arises especially from the condition of the proletariat, which is "a class with radical chains," and so "has a universal character by its universal [human] suffering." This class, therefore, represents "the *complete loss* of man and hence can win itself only through the *complete rewinning of man*." Otherwise put, given its all-around alienation, the proletariat is not only compelled to invoke "a human title" but also is the only class capable of invoking it universally and radically. Interestingly, Marx here sees a natural alliance between revolutionary philosophy (consciousness or theory) and the proletariat: "As philosophy finds its material weapons in the proletariat, so the proletariat finds its spiritual weapons in philosophy. And once the lightning of thought has squarely struck this ingenuous soil of the people the emancipation of ... [the whole society] into human beings will take place."[39]

In *The Holy Family*, Marx (and Engels) treats the proletariat itself as a potentially radical philosopher, which would necessarily develop its revolutionary consciousness from its own inhuman experience. In his wording, the proletariat "feels annihilated in estrangement; it sees in it its own powerlessness and the reality of an inhuman existence." In this "its abasement," the proletariat

---

[37] "Marx to Friedrich Bolte, November 23, 1871," 258-59.
[38] Marx, "Contribution to the Critique of Hegel's Philosophy of Right: Introduction," 182. Comments such as this have inspired some authors to detect a Kantian influence in Marx's writings. See, for instance, Karatani, *Transcritique: On Kant and Marx*, 130.
[39] Ibid., 186, 187.

develops its "indignation," "an *indignation* to which it is necessarily driven by the contradiction between its human *nature* and its condition of life, which is the outright, resolute and comprehensive negation of that nature." This is a prelude to revolutionary consciousness, based as it is on his humanist conscience, which is once again described as a (moral) categorical imperative.

> [S]ince man has lost himself in the proletariat, yet at the same time has not only gained theoretical consciousness of that loss, but through urgent, no longer removable, no longer disguisable, absolutely imperative need—the practical expression of necessity—is driven directly to revolt against this inhumanity, it follows that the proletariat can and must emancipate itself. But it cannot emancipate itself without abolishing the conditions of its own life. It cannot abolish the conditions of its own life without abolishing all the inhuman conditions of life of society today which are summed up in its own situation.[40]

However, at least for now, this consciousness belongs to Marx, not the proletariat itself. He thus concludes that "It is not a question of what this or that proletarian, or even the whole proletariat, at the moment *regards* as its aim. It is a question of *what the proletariat is*, and what, in accordance with this *being*, it will historically be compelled to do." Once again, "Its aim and historical action is visibly and irrevocably foreshadowed in its own life situation as well as in the whole organization of bourgeois society today."[41]

I now argue that the views presented in the preceding paragraphs of this section are compatible with the often-quoted claim, made in *The German Ideology*, that revolutionary consciousness would sooner or later arise. In the relevant discussion, Marx and Engels argue that with the development of productive forces in capitalism,

> a class [i.e. the proletariat] is called forth, which has to bear all the burdens of society without enjoying its advantages, which, ousted from society, is forced into the most decided

---

[40] Marx and Engels, *The Holy Family*, 37.
[41] Ibid.

antagonism to all other classes; a class which forms the majority of all members of society, and from which emanates the consciousness of the necessity of a fundamental revolution, the communist consciousness, which may, of course, arise among the other classes too through the contemplation of the situation of this class.[42]

The implied idea here, which is also repeated in the preceding paragraphs, is that "the consciousness of the necessity of a fundamental revolution," namely, "the communist consciousness," ultimately arises "through the contemplation of the situation" of the working class. If not the working class, or a sizeable portion of it, has not yet acquired it, Marx and Engels (members of "other classes") surely have. Their communist consciousness has arisen from the contemplation of the situation in which workers are compelled to "bear all the burdens of society without enjoying its advantages." If so, "the communist consciousness" issues from the recognition of the suffering (alienation) of the working class, who is in the process of acquiring this consciousness for itself.

We find similar thoughts in the "materialist" *Manifesto* about the link between the necessity of a fundamental revolution and the awareness of alienation. By developing the material conditions of production and commerce, Marx and Engels first argue, "the bourgeois ... has also called into existence the men who are to ... [overthrow it]—the modern working class—the proletarians." They then go on to adumbrate a host of reasons that collectively, so they maintain, necessitate this outcome. These include the facts that workers "live only so long as they find work, and who find work only so long as their labor increases capital"; they "must sell themselves piecemeal, [and so] are a commodity, like every other article of commerce, and are consequently exposed to all the vicissitudes of competition, to all the fluctuations of the market," cheapening the worth of labor and making the worker's existence increasingly precarious. Furthermore,

Masses of laborers, crowded into the factory, are organized like soldiers. As privates of the industrial army they are placed under the command of a perfect hierarchy of officers and

---

[42] Marx and Engels. *The German Ideology*, 52.

sergeants. Not only are they slaves of the bourgeois class, and of the bourgeois State; they are daily and hourly enslaved by the machine, by the overlooker, and, above all, by the individual bourgeois manufacturer himself. The more openly this despotism proclaims gain to be its end and aim, the more petty, the more hateful and the more embittering it is.[43]

The basis of Marx's revolutionary consciousness and conscience is most clearly articulated in the *Grundrisse* (1857-58) and the *Economic Manuscript of 1861-63*. The relevant passage from the *Grundrisse* reads:

The recognition [by the worker] of the products as ... [his/her] own, and the judgment that its separation from the conditions of ... [his/her] realization is improper [*ungehörig*] and forcibly imposed by force, is an enormous [advance in] consciousness, and is itself the product of the mode of production based on capital, and just as much the [death] KNELL TO ITS DOOM as the consciousness of the slave that he cannot be the *property of another*.[44]

This passage, which speaks for itself, is preceded by a consideration of some of the key aspects of alienation. In the second, almost identical passage, alienation is discussed in more detail, followed by the same articulation (likely copied from the one from the *Grundrisse*) of the consciousness that emerges from it logico-ethically. A very lengthy quotation is in order, not least because the following passage brings together much of what the present study is all about:

What is reproduced and newly produced [in the process of capital accumulation] is not only the *being* of these objective conditions of living labor but *their being as alien* to the worker, as independent values, i.e. values belonging to an alien subject [the capitalist], confronting this living labor capacity. The

---

[43] Marx and Engels, *Manifesto of the Communist Party*, 490-91.
[44] Marx, *Outlines of the Critique of Political Economy*, *MECW* 28: 390-91. All citations of those works that appear in multiple volumes of *Marx and Engels Collected Works* include the acronym *MECW*, followed by the relevant volume number.

objective conditions of labor gain a *subjective* existence as against living labor capacity—*capital* [logically] gives rise to the *capitalist*. On the other hand, the purely subjective being of labor capacity vis-à-vis its own conditions gives it a merely indifferent objective form as against these conditions—it [living labor] is [treated] only ... [as] *a commodity*—alongside its own conditions [of existence, namely] ... *other commodities*. Instead of being reproduced in the production process as conditions for ... [the capacities of living labor's] realization, they [other commodities] on the contrary emerge from it as conditions for their own valorization and preservation as values-for-themselves over against [living labor]. The material on which it [living labor] works is *alien* material; just as the instrument is an alien instrument; its labor appears as a mere accessory to them [the instruments] as substance and therefore objectifies itself in things not belonging to it. Indeed, living labor itself appears as alien vis-à-vis the living labor capacity whose labor it is, whose life it expresses, for it is surrendered to capital in return for objectified labor, for the product of labor itself. Labor capacity relates to it as to something alien, as *compulsory labor*. Its own labor is alien to it—and, as we see in capitalist production, it really *is* alien, as regards its content, its direction, and its social form—just as much as material and instrument are. Therefore, the product too appears to it as a combination of alien material, alien instrument and alien labor—as *alien property*, and after production it has become poorer by the life force expended, and it begins the DRUDGERY anew as labor capacity EMPLOYED by the *conditions of labor*. The recognition of the product as its own, and its awareness that its separation from the conditions of its realization is an injustice [*unrecht*]— *a relationship imposed by force*—is an enormous consciousness, *itself the product* of the capitalist mode of production and just as much the KNELL TO ITS DOOM as the consciousness of the slave that he could not be the property of another reduced slavery to an artificial, lingering existence, and made it impossible for it to continue to provide the basis of production.[45]

---

[45] Marx, *Economic Manuscript of 1861-63*, *MECW* 34: 245-46.

As Jon Elster aptly observes, the "injustice" perceived in this passage is "part of the motivation for abolishing it."[46] Clearly, it is Marx who everywhere reaches this communist-revolutionary consciousness, which he expects to "grip" the mass of workers sooner or later. Thus, we must assume, the motivation for abolishing capitalism belongs to Marx and those who agree with his conscience and consciousness. The ground for this motivation-consciousness is alienation, which entails dehumanization. Hence, and once more, "the *categorical imperative to overthrow all relations* in which man is debased, enslaved, forsaken, despicable being."[47]

***

Marx's inevitability argument cannot be taken seriously. It must thus be, and often is even by some of his reasonable followers, bracketed out. What remains are his categorical and hypothetical imperatives, which may be restated as a humanist-ethical justification of revolution and the necessity to make it in practice.

The ensuing two chapters consider the kind of revolution Marx sought to make and the last one the kind of society he sought to achieve by it. As Chapter 6 and (especially) Chapter 7 collectively illustrate, Marx had conceived revolution essentially as a gradual process of dealienation or self-emancipation. Chapter 8 shows that he conceived socialism as the positive transcendence of alienation.

---

[46] Elster, *Making Sense of Marx*, 106, 219.
[47] Marx, "Contribution to the Critique of Hegel's Philosophy of Right: Introduction," 182.

Revolutionary Gradualism

6.1 Introduction

His establishment opponents used to call Marx "the Red Doctor of Terror," falsely believing that he had orchestrated the Paris uprising of 1871. His voluntarist opponents, on the other hand, charged him with betraying the revolutionary cause. These images of him are both correct and false. As this chapter illustrates, excepting a brief period, Marx was generally a *revolutionary gradualist*.[1] His advocacy for the radical transformation of society, for the achievement of socialism, established his revolutionary credentials, while his strategy to achieve this goal slowly by democratic and other "normal" means qualified him as a gradualist.

6.2 first considers the period of exception, extending roughly from 1848-1849 to 1850, during which Marx (and Engels) had pursued a putschist strategy. It then goes on to illustrate his sharp departure from this strategy, complete withdrawal from political activity, and devotion to "theoretical" studies to discover capitalism's inevitable demise in its own "material conditions" and "law of motion." This reintroduced the evolutionist component of his earlier theory to his post-putschist theory of revolution.

Marx joined the International Working Men's Association in 1864, thus ending his political isolation. As a leader of the International, he had consistently opposed "the alchemists of revolution," and urged the development of working-class associations, preferably both under the aegis of the International and committed to the eventual emancipation of the working class (6.3).

6.4 documents how Marx's political strategy hinged on winning the struggle for democracy, which is informed by his conviction that universal suffrage would necessarily lead to the political supremacy of the working-class majority and, consequently, to socialism. However, this had to come to its own in tandem with the development of the material conditions in capitalism, which he expected to not only exhaust capitalism's development but also to establish the economic-technological preconditions for achieving socialism. Marx, in other words, never subscribed to the view that

---

[1] In constructing this and the next chapter, I found McLellan's *Karl Marx: His Life and Thought* very useful.

socialism could be achieved in places where capitalism was not already sufficiently developed.

In the final analysis, this chapter intends to provide an informative practical and biographical backdrop to the philosophical underpinnings of Marx's revolutionary gradualism, which will be considered in the next chapter.

6.2 From Revolutionary "Folly" to Inactivity

"For the oppressed class to be able to emancipate itself," Marx writes in *The Poverty of Philosophy* (1847), "it is necessary that the productive powers already acquired, and the existing social relations should no longer be capable of existing side by side." Therefore, "The organization of revolutionary elements [i.e., workers] as a class supposes the existence of all the productive forces which could be engendered in the bosom of the old society."[2]

The point I wish to make here is made by Marx's himself in an article he published at the heels of *The Poverty of Philosophy*: "If … the proletariat overthrows the political rule of the bourgeoisie, its victory will only be temporary" because "the material conditions have not yet been created which make necessary the abolition of the bourgeois mode of production and therefore also the definitive overthrow of the political rule of the bourgeoisie." "In the course of their development," he adds, the existing society must first "*produce the material conditions* of a new society …; no exertion of mind or will can free them from this fate.[3] I will henceforth refer to this as the "material-conditions argument."

In very short order, during the revolutionary upheavals of 1848, Marx and Engels came to believe that a proletarian revolution was imminent. The impending "bourgeois revolution in Germany," one reads in the *Manifesto* (written at the end of 1847 and the beginning of 1848), "will be but the prelude to an immediately following proletarian revolution."[4] Given their obvious commitment to the material-conditions argument in the *Manifesto*, this claim indicates that Marx and Engels believed at the time that such conditions were ripe in Germany, if not elsewhere. Not incidentally, this belief reveals the vagueness of the material-conditions argument, in that a

---

[2] Marx, *The Poverty of Philosophy*, 211.
[3] Marx, "Moralizing Criticism and Critical Morality," 319-20.
[4] Marx and Engels, *Manifesto of the Communist Party*, 519.

revolutionary situation could be regarded as the proof of the maturity of such conditions and its absence the contrary condition. Convinced as they were at the time of the immediacy of the impending proletarian revolution, Marx and Engels found themselves in strategic agreement with the "putschist" or "conspiratorial" Blanquists, with whom they had already formed the Communist League in 1847, parted company thereafter, and rejoined in 1849, agreeing that despite the recent defeat of the working class in 1849, the League could still organize a revolution successfully.

Thus, their March 1850 "Address" to the League, secretly disseminated for good reasons, declares that "a new revolution is impending"; it "is near at hand."[5] The "Address" also issues specific instructions, such as arming the working class, preventing its cooptation by the other parties, and engaging in terroristic means.[6] In short, its authors clearly appear to be plotting an armed insurrection in this document. Therefore, the claim that Marx and Engels were, at least during this brief period, in agreement with the Blanquists is not without merit.[7]

Apparently, as others have also noted, Marx and Engels had mistaken the birth pangs of modern capitalism for its death throes. However, when their efforts were decisively defeated in short order, their putschist and conspiratorial attitude fizzled away as rapidly as it had emerged. Thus, scarcely a month after circulating the "Address," Marx and Engels denounced all conspiratorial tendencies in their review of the recent literature on the revolution:

> It needs scarcely be added that these conspirators do not confine themselves to the general organizing of the revolutionary proletariat. It is precisely their business to

---

[5] Marx and Engels, "Address of the Central Authority to the League, March 1850," 278-79.

[6] Ibid., 283, 286-87.

[7] Indeed, the "Address" is the primary source of those who have declared them students of Blanqui. This view was popularized by Eduard Bernstein as early as 1898. For a discussion and critique, see Riazanov, "The Relations of Marx with Blanqui." For one of the most exhaustive discussions of this issue, see Hunt, *Marx and Engels*. Hunt's otherwise excellent study is blemished by his rather zealous attempt to disassociate Marx from Blanquist putschism even during this short period.

anticipate the process of revolutionary development, to bring it artificially to crisis-point, to launch a revolution on the spur of the moment, without the conditions for a revolution. For them the only condition for revolution is the adequate preparation of their conspiracy. They are the alchemists of the revolution ... Occupied with such scheming, they have no other purpose than the most immediate one of overthrowing the existing government and have the profoundest contempt for the more theoretical enlightenment of the proletariat about their class interests.[8]

Gradualism was now back on their agenda; it was time to break with "the alchemists of the revolution." This occurred *de facto* during a meeting with their Blanquist counterparts in the League, held in September 1850. Marx: "Whereas we say to the workers: You have 15, 20, 50 years of civil war to go through in order to alter the situation and to train yourselves for the exercise of power, it is said [by the Blanquists, etc.]: We must take power at once, or else we may as well take to our beds." If pressed, I suspect, Marx would have gone even higher than "50 years." "Our party," he went on to argue accordingly, "can come to power only when the conditions allow it to put its own views into practice."[9]

This is surely an argument in favor of opposing any revolution until "the conditions" for its success are ripe. But what did he mean by "revolution" in this context? Clearly, he meant a protracted process, during which the working class should "train" itself "for the exercise of power." This is a radically different strategy from the one that seeks training, as it were, for the *overthrow* of the existing power and order of things at an opportune moment. It entails the formation of the "sprouts" of the future society within capitalism itself, as we will see in the next chapter.

In any case, immediately thereafter, Marx and Engels isolated themselves from the "alchemists of the revolution," who were trying to regroup in England—where Marx himself had recently moved (in June 1849). In Marx's own words, posted to Engels on February 11, 1851, "I am greatly pleased by the public, authentic isolation in

---

[8] Marx and Engels, "*Les Conspirateurs, par A. Chenu ...*," 318.
[9] Marx, "Meeting of the Central Authority, September 15, 1850," 626, 628. Also see Marx and Engels, "Review, May to October (1850)," 510.

which we two, you and I, now find ourselves. It is wholly in accord with our attitude and our principles." His letter to Engels also confesses that their own flirtation with the recent conspiratorial projects entailed unwise compromises from their principles: "The system of mutual concessions, half-measures tolerated for decency's sake, and the obligation to bear one's share of public ridicule in the party along with all these jackasses, all this is now over."[10]

Thus, as Engels would recall many years later (1885), they hereafter "most decidedly refused to ... enter into the game of making revolutions." And, their "cool estimation of the situation ... was regarded as heresy among many persons," who were still playing "the game." Subsequently, in November 1852, writes Engels, "we dissolved our League."[11]

During this period, Marx also came to believe that there was not any reason to engage in political activity anyway. Indeed, this sentiment would last until the early 1860s, that is, even after his retrospective letter of February 29, 1860, to Ferdinand Freiligrath. "After the 'League' had been disbanded at my behest in November 1852," Marx writes in this letter, "I *never* belonged to any society again, whether *secret* or *public*; that the *party*, therefore, in this wholly ephemeral sense, ceased to exist for me 8 years ago." Marx's ensuing testimony is worth quoting at some length:

> You [Freiligrath] will recall that the leaders of the fairly ramified Communist Club in New York ... sent me a letter ... in which it was tentatively suggested that I should reorganize the old League. A whole year passed before I replied, and then it was to the effect that since 1852 I had not been associated with *any* association and was firmly convinced that my theoretical studies were of greater use to the working class than my meddling with associations which had now had their day on the Continent. Because of this 'inactivity' I was thereupon repeatedly and bitterly attacked ... [for] my 'doctrinaire' indifference ... Whereas you are a poet, I am a critic and for me the experiences of 1849-52 were quite enough.[12]

---

[10] "Marx to Frederick Engels, February 11, 1851," 118.
[11] Engels, "On The History of the Communist League," 327-29.
[12] "Marx to Ferdinand Freiligrath, February 29, 1860," 81-82.

As we have seen in Chapter 5, Marx certainly was not at any time in his adult life indifferent to the suffering of the proletariat; nor had he ever given up on the desideratum of a revolution—gradual or otherwise—to emancipate it. However, as we just learned, he had isolated himself from revolutionary activities and parties since 1852. His "theoretical studies" convinced him that the material conditions for a revolutionary transition to communism were not yet ripe.

One such study was his 1859 *Contribution*:

No social formation is ever destroyed before all the productive forces for which it is sufficient have been developed, and new superior relations of production never replace older ones before the material conditions for their existence have matured within the framework of the old society. Mankind thus inevitably sets itself only such tasks as it is able to solve.[13]

The last sentence of this passage should be read as a prescription. In any case, in another theoretical study, written a few years later (1861-1863), Marx goes so far as to liken epochal changes to slow geological movements: "Just as one should not think of sudden changes and sharply delineated period in considering the succession of the different geological formations, so also in the case of the creation of the different economic formations of society."[14] This evolutionist view would underpin his political gradualism during the ensuing years.

6.3 Marx, the Alchemists, and the International

However, during this period, new developments were signaling the revival of progressive politics, such as the revival of the working-class movements in France and the creation of The London Trades Council—a union of unions—in 1860. In addition, there was the Polish January Uprising in 1863.

"What do you think of the Polish business?" Marx asks in a letter to Engels. "This much is certain," he answers, "the era of revolution has now fairly opened in Europe once more ... This time,

---

[13] Marx, *A Contribution to the Critique of Political Economy*, 263.
[14] Marx, *Economic Manuscript of 1861-63, MECW* 33: 442.

let us hope, the lava will flow from East to West ..., so that we shall be spared the 'honor' of the French initiative." His reference to the French is informed by his collaboration with the alchemists of the revolution. "But the comfortable *delusions* and almost childish enthusiasm with which we welcomed the revolutionary era before February 1848, have gone by the board. We now know what role stupidity plays in revolutions ..."[15]

In short order, Marx found himself at the well-attended inaugural meeting of the International, held on September 28, 1864, "in a non-speaking capacity on the PLATFORM." The initiative for the meeting came from "London workers," who "some time ago" [in December 1863] sent an address to workers in Paris about Poland and called upon them to act jointly in the matter [of supporting the Polish uprising]."[16]Soon thereafter, the non-speaking attendee would become the guiding spirit of the International.

Under Marx's direction, the International adopted a revolutionary-gradualist program. In other words, the main-stream General Council (and Marx) of the International was revolutionary only in principle, for its chief aim was the self-emancipation of the working class. In its daily activities, however, it was essentially a normal class-politics steering committee, and so was gradualist in practice. The aim of this strategy was to mediate the training of the working class to rule itself, which meant suppressing the "French" conspiratorial, putschist strategy.

The general course the International would subsequently take is outlined in Marx's "Inaugural Address," which stresses three main points. The first point is captured in his opening statement: "It is a great fact that the misery of the working masses has not diminished from 1848 to 1864, and yet this period is unrivaled for the development of its industry and the growth of its commerce." The intended message here is that the emancipation of the working class cannot be fully attained within capitalism. The second point highlights "the failure of the Revolution of 1848" and the subsequent dismal "defeat of the continental working classes." Several factors are identified as the culprits responsible for this outcome, including the conspiratorial strategies of certain movements (read the League) during this period. The third point is made implicitly but clearly nevertheless: The gradualist strategies

---

[15] "Marx to Frederick Engels, February 13, 1863," 453.
[16] "Marx to Frederick Engels, November 4, 1864," 15-16.

of the working-class in England have been more successful than these adventuristic ones, such as the improvement of the working conditions and winning the struggle for the "the Ten Hours' Bill." A "still greater victory" however, "is the co-operative movement, especially the co-operative factories raised by the unassisted efforts of a few bold 'hands'. The value of these great [spontaneous] social experiments cannot be overrated."[17]

I will further discuss their value to Marx in Chapter 7. Suffice it to note here that Marx conceived them as the sprouts of self-emancipation and the future society. It is also clear that valuing them meant devaluing the putschist strategies of revolution. In short, he was now defending a gradualist strategy in practice as well.

This strategy was also informed by Marx's ongoing evolutionist economic determinism, which is clearly defended in his "Preface" to *Capital* (1867). In it, he brandishes "the economic law of motion of modern society" to both predict the inevitable abolition of capitalism and to explain why this cannot happen unless each society, in its divergent ways, goes through the necessary stages of economic development the "law" purportedly governs. Thus, every society must go through the necessary stages of development of capitalism, as England has and still is doing, before being able to successfully transcend it. "If, however, the German reader shrugs his shoulders at the condition of the English industrial and agricultural laborers, or in optimist fashion comforts himself with the thought that in Germany things are not nearly so bad," proclaims Marx, "I must plainly tell him, '*De te fabula narratur*'."[18]

In this context, Marx argues that the working class should still improve its lot by urging legislation and reform, pointing to England as a paradigmatic example of such successful strategies. In other words, "One nation [or society] can and should learn from others." Yet, a society "can neither clear by bold leaps, nor remove by legal enactments, the obstacles offered by the successive phases of its normal development," based as this is on "the natural laws of its movement." "But it can shorten and lessen the birth pangs" of the new society.[19] This is a recipe for political reformism, which regards

---

[17] Marx, "Inaugural Address of the Working Men's International Association," 5-13.

[18] Marx, *Capital*, Vol. 1, 10. Marx would later revise this stages-theory.

[19] Ibid.

only the material-economic forces as meaningfully revolutionary.

On January 1, 1870, Marx issued the following lines in a circular:

> Although revolutionary *initiative* will probably come from France, England alone can serve as the *lever* for a serious [and successful] *economic* Revolution. It is the only country where there are no more peasants and where landed property is concentrated in a few hands. It is the only country where the *capitalist form*, that is to say combined labor on a large scale under capitalist masters, embraces virtually the whole of production. It is the only country *where the great majority of the population consists of WAGES-LABORERS*. It is the only country where the class struggle and the organization of the working class by the *TRADES UNIONS* have *acquired* a certain degree of maturity and universality. It is the only country where, because of its domination on the world market, every revolution in economic matters must immediately affect the whole world. If landlordism and capitalism are classical features in England, on the other hand, the *material conditions* for their *destruction* are the most mature here.[20]

To clarify, Marx does not here maintain that England, or France for that matter, is ripe for a revolution. To say the least, a "spirit of generalization and revolutionary ardor" is lacking in England, and it is the aim of the International to help foster such a spirit and ardor. Although the point is not explicitly made, the context sufficiently clarifies that the revolutionary strategy Marx urges here is a gradualist one, based upon his usual economic evolutionism. "England," insists Marx accordingly, "cannot be treated simply as a country along with other countries. It must be treated as the metropolis of capital."[21]

In other words, the revolutionary character of Marx's strategy consists in its general, transformative "great end," repeated here as "the economical emancipation of the working classes" and "the abolition of all class rule."[22] It does not consist in plotting an

---

[20] Marx, "The General Council to the Federal Council of Romance Switzerland," 86.

[21] Ibid., 87

[22] Ibid., 87-90.

insurrection, and it is clear that Marx's disparagement of the non-revolutionary elements in this document has essentially to do with their refusal to commit themselves to these two related "great' aims.

Furthermore, the revolutionary *"initiative,"* to which Marx refers in the above passage, is related to the increased political agitation in France during the previous two years, which brought about the persecution of the members of the International. Through Marx's pen and wisdom, the International had repeatedly condemned such repressions and denied the charges that it was itself a conspiratorial organization. Such charges were not entirely groundless, however, for certain sects and individuals associated with the International were indeed involved in such "complot." Thus, Marx had to also denounce these alchemists of revolution.

An example of this is the July 7, 1868, resolution of the International to dissociate itself from the activities and declarations of one Félix Pyat, which was proposed by Marx. About a week earlier, at a public meeting to celebrate the anniversary of the June 1848 insurrection of the Paris workers, Pyat "delivered a speech and moved a provocative resolution urging terroristic acts against Napoleon III." The speech was printed in numerous newspapers, which rather unscrupulously associated Pyat and his resolution with the International, likely at the urging of Pyat himself.[23]

During this period, Marx was also keeping an eye on Michael Bakunin, the chief anarchist, who was a proponent of conspiratorial secret societies of revolutionists, waiting for the next opportunity to lead an insurrection. In his "The Program of the International Brotherhood" (1869), Bakunin thus defines proper revolution as "an outburst of what today is called 'evil passions' and the destruction of the so-called public order." Although this "popular revolution ... will create its revolutionary organization from the bottom up, from the circumference to the center," somehow it is still "necessary ... that the unity of ideas and of revolutionary action find an *organ* in the midst of the popular anarchy ... This organ should be *the secret and universal association of the International Brothers* ..., a sort of revolutionary general staff, composed of dedicated, energetic, intelligent individuals, sincere friends of the people." The great

---

[23] Marx, "Resolution of the General Council on Félix Pyatt's Provocative Behavior," 7. For the context, see the editors' note, *MECW* 21: 451.

alchemist of revolutions then estimates that "One hundred revolutionaries, strongly and earnestly allied, would suffice for the international organization of all of Europe." [24] In short, Bakunin called for a rapid destruction of the existing order of things.[25]

Naturally, Marx was not impressed by any of this, calling Bakunin "a nonentity as a theoretician," who is only "in his element as an intriguer."[26] In his 1874-1875 conspectus on Bakunin's *Statism and Anarchy*, Marx accordingly notes: "He understands absolutely nothing of social revolution, only its political rhetoric; its economic conditions simply do not exist for him." In the final analysis, "Willpower, not economic conditions, is the basis of his social revolution."[27] As we will see in the next section, Marx would soon wage a struggle against Bakunin and his supporters within the International, with the intention of expelling them.

With this context in mind, I now reiterate that Marx's January 1, 1870, praise for "the class struggle and the organization of the working class" in England was, at least in part, an expression of support for the English gradualist model over the "French" complot-putschist model. The preference needed to be stressed due to the continued appeal of the latter among, especially, the French revolutionaries. Consequently, due to the repetition of similar behavior by the London French Federal Branch, to which Pyat belonged, Marx's resolution to publicly sever all relationships with this association was adopted on May 10, 1870.[28]

The resolution was adopted shortly after another similar event, which was—and because it was—linked to the International in the press. The event, which took place on May 3 in London, was organized to honor Gustave Flourens, Marx's friend of longstanding, and a Blanquist initiator of a botched republican

---

[24] Bakunin, *Bakunin on Anarchy*, 151-55.
[25] "Revolution means war, and that implies the destruction of men and things. Of course, it is a pity that humanity has not yet invented a more peaceful means of progress, but until now every forward step in history has been achieved only after it has been baptized in blood." Bakunin, *The Political Philosophy of Bakunin*, 369-70, 372.
[26] "Marx to Friedrich Bolte, November 23, 1871," 255.
[27] Marx, "Notes on Bakunin's *Statehood and Anarchy*," 518.
[28] Marx, "Draft Resolution of the General Council on the 'French Federal Section in London'," 131.

uprising in Paris on February 7. Flourens would later play an important role in the creation of the Paris Commune of 1871 and would subsequently be killed during its defense—after refusing to surrender. Pyat was also involved in the Commune as one of its leading figures, though some scholars suggest that he had done more harm than good.[29]

It is thus not surprising that Marx would soon warn the members of the International to refrain from staging a revolution in France. This happened at the heels of the collapse of the Second Empire, immediately after Napoleon III's forces were defeated at Sedan on September 4 by the Prussians. The same day, the provisional government of the Third Republic of France, led by Adolphe Thiers, was proclaimed. Simultaneously, at the urging of the French members of the International, the idea for the formation of a socialist-democratic commune started to gain support, especially after the new government capitulated to the demands of the Prussians.

To make the long story short, Marx, who had almost no influence in France, opposed the idea. First, he did so privately in his letter of September 6, 1870, to Engels:

I had just "sat down" to write to you when Serraillier came to tell me that he is leaving London tomorrow for Paris, but only for a few days. His chief purpose is to arrange matters with the International there (*Conseil Fédéral de Paris*). This is all the more essential as the entire FRENCH BRANCH [led by Pyat and disowned by the International] is setting off for Paris today to commit all sorts of follies there in the name of the *International*. "They" intend to bring down the Provisional Government, establish a *commune de Paris*, nominate Pyat as French ambassador in London, and so forth.[30]

Three days later, Marx pleaded his case publicly:

Any attempt at upsetting the new [republican] government in the present crisis, when the enemy is almost knocking at the doors of Paris, would be a desperate folly. The French

---

[29] For a well-informed study, see Blaisdell, "Félix Pyat, the 'Evil Genius' of the Commune of Paris."
[30] "Marx to Frederick Engels, September 6, 1870," 64-65.

workmen must perform their duties as citizens; but, at the same time, they must not allow themselves to be swayed by the national *souvenirs* of 1792, as the French peasant allowed themselves to be deluded by the national *souvenirs* of the First Empire. They have not to recapitulate the past, but to build up the future. Let them calmly and resolutely improve the opportunities of republican liberty, for the work of their own class organization. It will gift them with fresh herculean powers for the regeneration of France, and our common task— the emancipation of labor. Upon their energies and wisdom hinges the fate of the republic.[31]

Clearly, Marx was urging calm and patience, understanding well that the working class was not yet ready, the French bourgeoisie and the Thiers government would not allow the proposed socialist commune to survive, and Bismarck would surely assist them. His worries were further confirmed by Engels, who informed him that a workers' uprising would "be needlessly crushed by the German armies and thrown back another twenty years."[32] Alas, it did not help to learn that Bakunin had in the meanwhile staged a botched revolution in Lyon and issued "most foolish decrees on the *abolition de l'état* and similar nonsense."[33] Against Marx's wishes, the Paris Commune was formally proclaimed on March 28, 1871, ten days after a rebellion broke out in the city against the new government and two days after the Parisians elected their delegates to the Commune.[34] In short order, Marx's warnings would turn into a nightmarish prophecy. Thus, soon thereafter, Bismarck released the captive French troops to help the new French government crush the Commune in what turned out to be one of the bloodiest repressions of an uprising in history. By May 28, it was all over. Marx, we are reasonably certain, fell into depression, as the news of bloodshed from Paris reached him.[35]

---

[31] Marx, "Second Address of the General Council ," 269.

[32] "Engels to Karl Marx, September 12, 1870," 71.

[33] "Marx to Edward Spencer Beesly, October 19, 1870," 88-89.

[34] See, among others, Edwards, *The Paris Commune, 1871*; Schulkind, *The Paris Commune of 1871*; Tombs, *The Paris Commune of 1871*; Merriman, *Massacre: The Life and Death of the Paris Commune of 1871*. Also see Gogol, *Toward a Dialectic of Philosophy and Organization*, 65-87.

[35] Jenny Marx: "The present state of things causes our dear Mohr [Marx] intense suffering and no doubt is one of the chief causes of his illness. A

Marx was neither surprised by any of this nor about to publicly blame the Communards for this portended disaster. Instead, in his *The Civil War in France* (a.k.a. "The Third Address"), he exalts the virtues of the Commune: "Working men's Paris, with its Commune, will be forever celebrated as the glorious harbinger of a new society. Its martyrs are enshrined in the great heart of the working class. Its exterminators, history has already nailed to that eternal pillory from which all the prayers of their priests will not avail to redeem them."[36]

Still, Marx remained convinced that the Parisian working class was not sufficiently developed to seize political power for itself, pointing out even in *The Civil War in France* that "in order to work out their own emancipation, and along with it that higher form to which present society is irresistibly tending by its own economical agencies ..., [workers] will have to pass through long struggles."[37] Indeed, he would remain convinced even a decade later that he was correct all-along: "The Paris Commune ... was merely an uprising of one city in exceptional circumstances," and "the majority of the Commune was in no sense socialist, nor could it have been." For this reason, the uprising defied "commonsense."[38]

Marx wrote these lines with the activities of his restless French supporters in mind. In late 1880, Jules Guesde and Paul Lafargue (Marx's son-in-law) met with Marx and Engels at Marx's residence to write the program of the newly-formed *Parti Ouvrier*. In his November 5, 1880 letter to Sorge, Marx describes the program, mainly written by him, as a "a tremendous step forward" in terms of bringing "the French workers down to earth out of their verbal cloud-cuckoo land." For this reason, and unsurprisingly, the program has "aroused much resentment among all those French intellectual frauds who make a living as 'cloud-assemblers'."[39] I will have more to say on this program in the next chapter.[40]

---

great number of friends are in the Commune. Some of them have already fallen victims to the butchers of Versailles." Quoted in Marx and Engels, *Writings on the Paris Commune*, 222.

[36] Marx, *The Civil War in France,* 355.

[37] Ibid, 335. Also see Marx, "First Draft of *The Civil War in France*," 491.

[38] "Marx to Ferdinand Domela Nieuwenhuis, February 22, 1881," 66.

[39] "Marx to Friedrich Adolph Sorge, November 5, 1880," 44.

[40] For a first-hand account of its composition, see "Engels to Eduard Bernstein, October 25, 1881," 148-49.

However, as Bernard H. Moss informs us, unlike Marx, "Guesde regarded … [it] not as a practical program of struggle, but simply as a means of agitation." The inevitable rejection of its demands by the bourgeoisie, Guesde believed, would "'free the proletariat of its last reformist illusions and convince it of the impossibility of avoiding a workers [17]89."[41] Consequently, like Marx, Engels saw in Guesde a man of "boundless impatience …, absolutely determined to see something worthwhile happen before he goes [dies]." This, he writes to Eduard Bernstein in his letter of October 25, 1881, explains "his exaggerated and sometimes destructive thirst for action."[42] For good reasons, Marx's famous statement, "'*Ce qu'il y a de certain c'est que moi, je ne suis pas Marxiste*' ['If anything is certain, it is that I myself am not a Marxist']," is assumed to be a reaction to the kind of "Marxism" represented in France by the likes of Guesde and Lafargue.[43]

6.4 Winning the Struggle for Democracy

The preceding pages, it is hoped, have firmly established Marx's revolutionary gradualism. However, at least two related questions remain unanswered in this context. One of them has to do with his approach to revolutionary violence. On this issue, I wish to make only a few quick remarks. To begin with, Marx had never developed a philosophy of "just war." Circa 1848, he (and Engels) thought the revolution to topple capitalism would necessarily be violent, for all revolutions were violent by their very nature. Subsequently, he came to believe that peaceful revolutions could possibly occur in certain countries. On several occasions, he expressed his preference for a peaceful revolution, if it could be had at all. On other occasions, he advocated violence against violence.[44] However, and again excepting the brief "Blanquist" period, he had never in his life incorporated the strategy of a forceful-violent overthrow of capitalism into his political programs.

The second question pertains to Marx's own gradualist strategy. His strategy, I argue, generally entailed what I call

---

[41] Moss, *The Origins of the French Labour Movement, 1830-1914*, 107.
[42] "Engels to Eduard Bernstein, October 25, 1881," 148-49.
[43] "Engels to Eduard Bernstein, November 2-3, 1882," 356.
[44] For a rich survey of Marx's comments on revolutionary violence, see Singh, "Status of Violence in Marx's Theory of Revolution."

"winning the struggle for democracy." This strategy overlapped with his revolutionary gradualism, in the sense that he had consistently linked it with the struggle for socialism. It was also informed by the material-conditions argument, it goes without saying. This section attempts to illustrate his commitment to gradual revolution by democratic means.

Skipping some earlier, relevant statements, we discover rudimentary elements of this strategy in the July 1846 "Address of the German Democratic Communists of Brussels to Mr. Feargus O'Connor," signed by Marx, Engels, and Philippe Gigot. The "Address" was meant to publicly congratulate this Chartist leader on winning a seat in the Parliament. According to its three authors, "'a democratic reconstruction of the Constitution upon the basis of the People's Charter'" will enable "the working class ... [to] become the ruling class of England."[45] A "working-class democracy" is at hand.[46]

The same strategy—or predilection, if one prefers—is revealed in Marx's September 1847 article, written primarily to expose the fake communism of an agent of the Prussian state, "Herr Consistorial Counsellor," who claimed in an article of his own that "it is not the liberal bourgeoisie but the government which represents the interests of the proletariat."[47] As we will see in the next chapter, Marx counters this claim with the argument that the proletariat needs to emancipate itself. What concerns us here is the aforesaid strategy, which Marx articulates thus:

[The proletariat] asks whether the present political system, the rule of the bureaucracy, or ... the [liberal-democratic] rule of the bourgeoisie will offer it the means to achieve its own purposes. To this end it only has to compare the political position of the proletariat in England, France and America with that in Germany to see that the rule of the bourgeoisie does not only place quite new weapons in the hands of the proletariat for the struggle against the bourgeoisie, but that it also secures for it a quite different status, the status of a recognized party.

---

[45] Marx and Engels, "Address of the German Democratic Communists of Brussels to Mr. Feargus O'Connor," 58.
[46] Ibid., 59.
[47] Marx, "The Communism of the *Rheinischer Beobachter*," 220.

Does the Herr Consistorial Counsellor then believe that the proletariat, which is more and more adhering to the Communist Party ..., will be incapable of utilizing the freedom of the press and the freedom of association? Let him just read the English and French working men's newspapers, let him just attend some time a single Chartist meeting![48]

Marx and Engels argue in the *Manifesto* (1848) that "the first step in the revolution by the working class is to raise the proletariat to the position of ruling class, *to win the battle of democracy* [emphasis added]."[49] What this statement means is not very clear, since the *Manifesto* also predicts that the projected revolution would entail violence. However, in his "Introduction" to the 1895 printing of Marx's *The Class Struggles in France*, Engels maintains that the statement in "*The Communist Manifesto*" refers to "the winning of universal suffrage, of democracy, as one of the first and most important tasks of the militant proletariat." In the hands of the workers' parties, he also adds retrospectively, "the franchise has been ... transformed ... from a means of deception, which it was heretofore, into an instrument of emancipation." In addition to giving many examples of the sense in which this has been the case, Engels contrasts this democratic path to socialism very favorably against the "wrong" putschist stance he and Marx had taken during the 1848-1850 upheavals.[50]

In an anticipatory manner, Marx also reiterated the same conclusion in his "The Chartists," published in *The New York Daily Tribune* in August 1852. By this time, he had reverted to the 1847 position discussed above, that is, to the advocacy for the gradualist struggle of the working class, citing specifically the Chartists' ("the politically active portion of the British working class") fight for the universal suffrage in England.

Universal Suffrage is the equivalent for political power for the working class of England, where the proletariat forms the large majority of the population, where, in a long, though

---

[48] Ibid., 222, 225.
[49] Marx and Engels, *Manifesto of the Communist Party*, 504.
[50] Engels, "Introduction (to Marx's *The Class Struggles in France, 1848 to 1850*)," 515-16.

underground [or disguised] civil war [i.e., class struggles], it has gained a clear consciousness of its position as a class .... The carrying of Universal Suffrage in England would, therefore, be a far more socialistic measure than anything which has been honored with that name on the Continent. Its inevitable result, here [in England], is *the political supremacy of the working class.*[51]

The main point of this passage is crystal clear. We also know from the preceding sections of this chapter that it is embedded in the evolutionist material-conditions argument, meaning that Marx does not here anticipate the political triumph of the working class anywhere in short order. What needs to be clarified is its application to "the Continent," especially France. Among other things, Marx observes in this regard that "the British Bourgeois are not excitable Frenchmen."[52] This quick observation contrasts the gradualism of the former with the putschist inclinations of the latter, a contrast that he here seems to derive from their cultural differences, as well as from their different levels of economic and political development.

In England, Marx further reasons, the capitalists do not have to wage a struggle against the relatively subdued state. Their main opponents are the other classes. Although the capitalists may at times appeal to the support of the working class against the aristocracy, their more threatening enemy is the working class; "if the aristocracy is their vanishing opponent the working class is their arising enemy." Therefore, the capitalists "prefer to compromise with the vanishing opponent rather than to strengthen the arising enemy, to whom the future belongs." Marx anticipates that, despite this, the bourgeoisie is compelled to "battering to pieces Old England, the England of the Past," and so to win "exclusive political dominion" for itself. In so doing, it will unite "political dominion [state power] and economical supremacy" in its hands. Consequently, "the [working-class'] struggle against capital [based on democratic means] will no longer be distinct from the struggle against the existing Government—from that very moment will date the *social revolution of England.*"[53]

---

[51] Marx, "The Chartists," 335-36.
[52] Ibid., 335.
[53] Ibid.

These conditions, Marx maintains, explain why universal suffrage would more readily, if not "inevitably," bring about "*the political supremacy of the working class*" in England than is the case in France. In the latter, due to its own peculiar historical conditions, etc., the configuration of the main forces is different. In France exists the massive, relatively independent, bureaucratic state machinery as an autonomous power, alongside the bourgeoise and the working class, though the sizeable smallholding peasantry is also politically pertinent. The aristocracy is no longer a crucial factor.

Consequently, as Marx further reiterates in *The Eighteenth Brumaire* (1852), the struggle for democracy in France faces certain additional hurdles. Specifically, he highlights how the French bourgeoisie "understood that all the so-called civil freedoms and organs of progress attacked and menaced its class rule at its social foundation and its political summit simultaneously and had therefore become 'socialistic'. In this menace and this attack, it *rightly* discerned the secret of socialism [emphasis added]."

> Thus, by now stigmatizing as '*socialistic*' what it had previously extolled as '*liberal*', the bourgeoisie confesses that its own interests dictate that it should be delivered from the danger of its own rule; that, in order to restore tranquility in the country, its bourgeois parliament must, first of all, be laid to rest; that, in order to preserve its social power intact, its political power must be broken [or abdicated to the bureaucratic state, in this case, led by the farcical Bonaparte]; that the individual bourgeois can continue to exploit the other classes and to enjoy undisturbed property, family, religion and order only on condition that their class be condemned along with the other classes to similar political nullity.[54]

Therefore, the situation on the ground has compelled the French bourgeoisie to be satisfied with "parliamentary cretinism,"[55] to abdicate its political power to the autonomous-bureaucratic state, to accept "*the victory of Bonaparte over the parliament, of the executive power over the legislative power.*" Thus, "before the

---

[54] Ibid, 142-43.
[55] Marx, *The Eighteenth Brumaire of Louis Bonaparte*, 161, 179.

executive power [the bourgeoisie] renounces all will of its own and submits to the superior command of an alien will, to authority."[56] Rather than dismissing the struggle for democracy in France as futile, Marx maintains here that if fully implemented, it would lead to socialism, though this would have to mean the abolition of the bureaucratic state as well. This explains why he thought the transition to socialism would likely be more violent in France than England, though calling for a violent putsch was not his strategy.

As noted in the previous section, Marx had withdrawn from political activities from 1852 to 1864. As also noted, he changed his mind and joined the International in 1864. What interests us in the present context is not only the revolutionary-gradualist strategy he would henceforth urge the International and its members to adopt but also how this meant combining the struggle for democracy with the socialistic-revolutionary aim of the emancipation of workers.

This strategy dovetails his advice to the French workers on September 9, 1870, to support the newly proclaimed Third Republic. To requote, "Let them calmly and resolutely improve the opportunities of republican liberty, for the work of their own class organization ... *Vive la République!*"[57]

After the Commune was defeated, Marx delivered his "Third Address," namely, *The Civil War in France*. In it, he converts the democratic-republican, pre-revolution "opportunities" to post-revolution desiderata. Thus, he writes approvingly, "Instead of deciding once in three or six years which member of the ruling class was to misrepresent the people in Parliament, universal suffrage was to serve the people, constituted in Communes, as individual suffrage serves every other employer in the search for the workmen and managers in his business."[58] As we will see in Chapter 8, this meant that Marx thought of socialism as a democratic system. Here, I stress that the logic of both the pre- and post-revolution appeals to the benefits of democratic-republican institutions is the same: They are both the proper and necessary political means to achieve socialism.

Winning the struggle for democracy entailed the strategy to make the working-class parties victorious. Thus, at The Hague

---

[56] Ibid., 184-85.
[57] Marx, "Second Address of the General Council of the International Working Men's Association on the Franco-Prussian War," 269.
[58] Marx, *The Civil War in France*, 333.

congress of the International in 1872, Marx campaigned for, and succeed in passing, three important resolutions, all related to the "secret" activities of Bakunin and the anarchist Alliance he led. First, the seat of the International was to be moved to New York, clearly with the intention of preventing the Bakuninist opposition, the "minority" present at The Hague Congress, from controlling the International. Second, Bakunin and one of his key allies, James Guillaume, were expelled from the International, and this after the augmented authority of the General Council to expel the anarchist sects from the International. Third, the Congress adopted the former's resolution to help organize the working class into a political party, raising it to political supremacy being its explicit aim.

This resolution, written by Marx and Engels, was adopted at the London Conference, held in September 1871, which pointed out that it was consistent with the previous resolutions of the International. It was adopted at the Hague Congress a year later. Its relevant sections read:

> In its struggle against the collective power of the propertied classes, the working class cannot act as a class except by constituting itself into a political party ... This constitution of the working class into a political party is indispensable in order to insure the triumph of the social revolution, and of its ultimate end, the abolition of classes ... [I]ts economical struggles ought, at the same time, to serve as a lever for its struggles against the political power of landlords and capitalists ..., [who] will always use their political privileges [to perpetuate] ... for the enslavement of labor. The conquest of political power has therefore become the great duty of the working class.[59]

Although this was already written on the wall before the Congress, the three resolutions made the split of the International into two "real" Internationals inevitable. The *de facto* split occurred a week later when Bakunin's anarchist allies summoned the St. Imier Congress. They rejected all the resolutions of the Congress of The Hague, accusing Marx and his followers of "German"

---

[59] Marx and Engels, "Resolutions of the General Congress Held at The Hague," 243.

authoritarian centralism, and of unbecoming personal intrigues against Bakunin and others. In addition, they adopted five resolutions of their own. The first resolution calls for "the autonomy and independence of the workers' federation and sections." The second resolution dovetails the first, basing the International on a "pact of friendship, solidarity, and mutual defense," and this against the "authoritarian party" of Marx. The third resolution targets the Marxist resolution to organize the proletariat into a political party, with the aim of conquering *political power*. It is based on the rather confused notion that "no political organization can be other than the organization of domination to the profit of one class and to the detriment of the masses, and that the proletariat, if it wishes to take power, would itself become a ruling, exploiter class." The fourth resolution basically advocates "an insurrection to destroy all political power." The fifth resolution amounts to an invitation for others to join this International.[60] The two Internationals would fizzle away and eventually disappear during the ensuing five years.[61]

However, Marx remained involved in the development of the working-class parties, as the next chapter further elaborates. With his involvement in the writing of "The Program of the *Parti Ouvrier*" in mind, suffice it to point out here that his idea of a revolutionary political party had remained consistent with the idea of winning the struggle for democracy.

Thus, we read the following in the preamble of this program, written by Marx in 1880:

> Considering,
> That this collective appropriation [of the means of production] can arise only from the revolutionary action of the productive class—or proletariat—organized in a distinct political party;
>
> That a such an organization must be pursued by all the means the proletariat has at its disposal including universal suffrage which will thus be transformed from the instrument of

---

[60] libcom.org/history/st-imier-congress-anti-authoritarian-international.

[61] For a recent, very rich account, which somewhat one-sidedly mainly blames Marx and Engels for the collapse of the International, see Eckhardt, *The First Socialist Schism*. For a similar perspective, see Berthier, *Social-Democracy and Anarchism*. For a more favorable portrayal of Marx, see Marcello Musto (ed.), *Workers Unite! The International 150 Years Later*.

deception that it has been until now into an instrument of emancipation;

The French socialist workers … have decided, as a means of organization and struggle, to enter the elections with the following immediate demands:

The political demands of the "Program," which are specific to France, stress the call for further democratization, including the "Abolition of all laws over the press, meetings and associations and above all the law against the International Working Men's Association," and making local communes (governments) the "master of its administration and its police."[62] Given the emphasis on universal suffrage and the other democratic demands, it is difficult to imagine that by "revolutionary action" Marx meant an insurrection. Indeed, and to recall, he saw the "Program" as a check against the "French intellectual frauds who make a living as 'cloud-assemblers'."[63]

***

As we have seen, winning the struggle for democracy was an essential aspect of Marx's revolutionary gradualism, as was the economic-material-conditions argument. Surely, this strategy was often guided by purely tactical questions, having much to do with the feasibility of successfully abolishing the existing order. However, it is evident that it also had to do with urging workers to train themselves "for the exercise of power," both economic and political. This idea is related to Marx's understanding of revolution as a gradual process of self-emancipation, which is informed by his humanist ethics.

---

[62] "The Program of the *Parti Ouvrier*."
https://www.marxists.org/archive/marx/works/1880/05/parti-ouvrier.htm
[63] "Marx to Friedrich Adolph Sorge, November 5, 1880," 44.

The Principle of Self-Emancipation as Dealienation

7.1 Introduction

Self-emancipation is the most fundamental principle of Marx's theory of revolution, as this chapter illustrates. His subscription to it is nowadays widely acknowledged, though the principle is often reduced to its practical aspect, to the simple claim that the working class must seize political power through its own efforts and use it to emancipate itself *from* the external causes of its unfreedom. This reading ignores the philosophical ground of the principle, and so falls short of adequately comprehending its deeper significance. As this chapter illustrates, Marx understood self-emancipation essentially as a process of self-dealienation.

7.2 draws crucial insights from Marx's early writings, with the aim of establishing the link he had consistently made between dealienation and self-emancipation. 7.3 illustrates how he insisted on making self-emancipation of the working class the cardinal principle of the International. As it is the case with the remaining sections of this chapter, 7.3 also throws into sharp relief the link Marx had consistently established between the concepts of self-emancipation and dealienation. 7.4 has similar aims, though it mainly focuses on Marx's application of the principle to workers' parties, especially in Germany and France. 7.5 examines his various discussions of the "sprouts" of the future society, such as workers' co-operatives and the peasant communes in Russia. Consequently, the chapter illustrates a crucial sense in which, in Marx's view, "the abolition of the capitalist mode of production [begins] within the capitalist mode of production itself."[1]

7.2 Early Formulations of the Principle

I will not repeat the details of Marx's theory of alienation. Suffice it to recall that it captures various modalities in which individuals, particularly workers, are unfree in capitalism. It thus follows that dealienation is understood as a process of regaining freedom, that is, as emancipation from the conditions, relations, and

---

[1] Marx, *Capital*, Vol. 3, 436.

processes of alienation. The idea this chapter attributes to Marx is basically that dealienation must issue directly from the activity of the alienated—just as alienation ultimately results from the activity of the same. This section illustrates the presence of this idea in Marx's early works.[2]

Let us begin with the young Marx's defense of democracy and various freedoms associated with it. For instance, in a 1842 article, he opposes censorship on the ground that "Freedom of the will is inherent in human nature [or essence]." The appeal to human essence appears many times in this article on the ongoing debates on freedom of the press. The following three statements are telling examples of such appeals: "Freedom is so much the essence of man that even its opponents implement it while combating its reality"; "it is envy which wants to abolish the eternal aristocracy of human nature, freedom"; "Is there no universal human nature, as there is a universal nature of plants and stars?"[3] The upshot: Freedom of expression, for instance, is a human good, and so should not be restricted by the authorities.[4]

The more directly relevant point for our present purposes emerges when Marx rebuts the argument of an opponent of freedom of the press—that human beings are naturally in need of restriction and guidance from above. He rephrases his argument to say, "true education consists in keeping a person wrapped up in a cradle throughout his life."[5] Marx here attempts to show how this argument leads to insurmountable contradictions. However, his ensuing rebuttal also implies that human beings, in accordance with their nature, must be allowed to develop or flourish freely. Top-down, bureaucratic control and management of a person's life is antithetical to this.

In his 1843 notes on, and disparaging critique of, Hegel's *Philosophy of Right*, Marx puts the same idea to a different use,

---

[2] For an interesting discussion, see Draper, *Karl Marx's Theory of Revolution: State and Bureaucracy*, 213-34.

[3] Marx, "Proceedings of the Sixth Rhine Province Assembly. First Article," 137, 155, 168, 191.

[4] These "are underpinned by a thick set of normative or even *ontological* considerations," not "pragmatic and utilitarian" ones. Hudis, *Marx's Concept of the Alterative to Communism*, 44.

[5] Marx, "Proceedings," 153,

arguing against the anti-democratic Hegel that in democracy, "the constitution is constantly brought back to its actual basis, the actual human being, the actual people, and established as the people's own work."[6] In other words, genuine (political) freedom is only possible in a democratic constitution,[7] which requires the abolition of the kind of bureaucratic-monarchical state (read the "Prussian state") Hegel glorifies in his *Philosophy of Right*.[8]

Marx's defense of democracy is thus predicated upon the idea that meaningful political freedom must issue from the will of the citizens. The reverse is at best abstract, alienated freedom. According to Marx, although he pretends to give it a philosophical wrap in his book, Hegel in fact borrows his idea of freedom from "the actual modern conditions, which presuppose the separation of real life from the life of the state and make belonging to a state an 'abstract definition' of the real member of the state."[9]

As we have seen in Chapter 3, Marx refers to this "separation" as the "twofold life" of the individual in "On the Jewish Question." To requote, "Where the political state has attained its true development, man—not only in thought, in consciousness, but in reality, in life—leads a twofold life," one "in the political community" and the other "in civil society, in which he acts as a private individual, regards other men as a means, degrades himself into a means, and becomes the plaything of alien powers."[10]

The "free state" Bauer defends is the state which grants and secures the "rights of man and of citizen." Although, as noted in Chapter 3, Marx problematically disparages "the rights of man" *tout court* as nothing but expressions of egoism, his assessment of citizenship rights is more positive. In any case, he refers to both types of rights as the bases of "political emancipation," which, he argues, "is, of course, a big step forward." However, it amounts only to the maximum "form of human emancipation" possible in modern society, "not the final form of human emancipation in general … It goes without saying that we are speaking here of real, practical

---

[6] Marx, "Contribution to the Critique of Hegel's Philosophy of Law," 29.
[7] Ibid., 29ff.
[8] Ibid., 121. Hegel's sycophantic defense of the Prussian state is amply illustrated in my *Hegel's Career and Politics*.
[9] Marx, "Contribution to the Critique of Hegel's Philosophy of Law," 115.
[10] Marx, "On the Jewish Question," 154.

emancipation."[11]

Rather than democracy *simpliciter*, Marx's remedy for alienation-unfreedom in this context is general self-emancipation (dealienation), the fulfilment of which would bring about communism, "the final form of human emancipation in general."

> Only when the real, individual man re-absorbs in himself the abstract citizen, and as an individual human being has become a species-being in his everyday life, in his particular work, and in his particular situation, only when man has recognized and organized his [own forces] as social forces, and consequently no longer separates social power from himself in the shape of political power, only then will human emancipation have been accomplished.[12]

The preceding passages all point to the same idea: dealienation must result from self-emancipation, which explicitly becomes the self-emancipation of the *proletariat* in his "Contribution to the Critique of Hegel's Philosophy of Law: Introduction." In this article, Marx describes the proletariat as "a class with radical chains ..., which cannot emancipate itself without emancipating" the entire society.[13]

While these lines went into print, Marx was writing the *Economic and Philosophic Manuscripts of 1844* in Paris. To state the obvious, the theory of alienation finds its most detailed articulation in this work. He also argues in it that "It takes actual communist action to abolish actual private property," which abolition he links with the abolition of various forms of alienation associated with private property (in the means of production). Interestingly, he expects this "communist action" to be "a very rough and protracted process." Thus, he does not conceive it as a rapid insurrection. Instead, almost intuitively, his mind immediately recalls the actions of the radical French workers and their associations, which he had directly observed while living in Paris. "When communist artisans associate with one another," he writes,

---

[11] Ibid., 155.

[12] Ibid., 168.

[13] Marx, "Contribution to the Critique of Hegel's Philosophy of Law: Introduction," 186.

"theory, propaganda, etc., is their first end." He then goes on to formulate a version of the sprout-theory:

> But at the same time, as a result of this association, they acquire a new need—the need for society—and what appears as a means becomes an end. In this practical process the most splendid results are to be observed whenever French socialist workers are seen together. Such things as smoking, drinking, eating, etc., are no longer means of contact or means that bring them together. Association, society and conversation, which again has association as its end, are enough for them; the brotherhood of man is no mere phrase with them, but a fact of life, and the nobility of man shines upon us from their work-hardened bodies.[14]

In short, Marx here discovers both self-emancipatory revolutionary action and the seeds of communist society in workers' associations. This discovery is the practical expression of Marx's dialectical formulation of communism as "the negation of the negation" in the same *Manuscripts*, that is, the negation (sublation) of alienation, which is the negation of human essence. Accordingly, he describes communism as the "next historical stage of development in the process of human emancipation and rehabilitation." Therefore, he calls communism "humanism."[15]

Leaving the issue of associations aside for now, we detect in these comments Marx's understanding of self-emancipation as the spontaneous activity of workers. If it was not already, this understanding would henceforth become his standpoint. He uses this very standpoint in *The Holy Family* (1845) to criticize Bauer's elitist depiction of ordinary people ("the mass") as "the passive, spiritless, unhistorical, *material* element of history," and the intellectuals, such as himself (a.k.a. "the Spirit'), "as the active element from which all *historical* action proceeds."[16] Against this view, Marx asserts that

> since the conditions of life of the proletariat sum up all the conditions of life of society today in their most inhuman form; since man has lost himself in the proletariat, yet at the same

---

[14] Marx, *Economic and Philosophic Manuscripts of 1844*, 313.
[15] Ibid., 306.
[16] Marx and Engels, *The Holy Family*, 86.

time has not only gained theoretical consciousness of that loss, but through urgent, no longer removable, no longer disguisable, absolutely imperative need—the practical expression of necessity—is driven directly to revolt against this inhumanity, it follows that the proletariat can and must emancipate itself.[17]

Alas, the argument is not without logical leaps and self-assuring presuppositions. Nevertheless, it does illustrate Marx's opposition to the elitist notions of emancipating the masses and, therefore, his own commitment to the principle of self-emancipation. This, in turn, is once again understood as emancipation from the conditions of alienation. Revolution is consequently defined as a "revolt against … inhumanity."

The principle of self-emancipation also finds a succinct expression in Marx's "Theses on Feuerbach" (1845). Indeed, the principle is arguably the main thesis of the "Theses." Accordingly, the third thesis states: "The materialist doctrine concerning the changing of circumstances and upbringing forgets that circumstances are changed by men and that the educator must himself be educated." This is a swipe at those, such as Robert Owen, who believe that a few enlightened individuals need to educate and emancipate the uneducated workers. "This doctrine," therefore, inevitably divides "society into two parts, one of which is superior to society." To the contrary, maintains Marx, "the changing of circumstances and of human activity or self-change" must coincide and take the form of "*revolutionary practice*."[18] Unlike what is often supposed, this "*practice*" or "*praxis*" does not refer to a political upheaval. Rather, it refers to a broader process of changing the world by those regarded as the "inferior" part of society, which crucially entails "self-change" as well. Indeed, self-emancipation is conceived essentially as self-change, not simply as emancipation *from* external factors and oppressors—such as the ruling class.

This view is stated more forcefully in the following passage from *The German Ideology* (1846), which clearly dovetails the third thesis:

---

[17] Ibid., 36-37.
[18] Marx, "Theses on Feuerbach," 4.

Both for the production on a mass scale of this communist consciousness, and for the success of the cause itself, the alteration of men on a mass scale is necessary, an alteration which can only take place in a practical movement, a *revolution*; the revolution is necessary, therefore, not only because the *ruling* class cannot be overthrown in any other way, but also because the class *overthrowing* it can only in a revolution succeed in ridding itself of all the muck of ages and become fitted to found society anew.[19]

Several crucial aspects of this passage are worth underlining. First, revolution is primarily understood as "a practical movement" during, and by, which "communist consciousness" is expected to arise. Second, and relatedly, the movement in question entails the self-alteration of workers ("men") "on a mass scale," meaning that changing the world is inextricably intertwined with self-change. Third, in "ridding itself of all the muck of ages,"[20] the self-emancipators "become fitted to found society anew."

The principle of the self-emancipation of the working class had by now become Marx's (and Engels') main motto. Although not the main topic of its interest, it reappears visibly in the last section of Marx's *The Poverty of Philosophy* (1847), titled "Strikes and Combinations of Workers." Here, Marx defends the ordinary class-struggles of the organized workers against not only the "economists," who tell workers that their efforts are ultimately futile, but also the utopian socialists, who instruct workers to adopt their enlightened schemes—to be emancipated by them. Marx implies in this context that workers are disabusing themselves of *all the muck of ages* through their own struggles and combinations, becoming a "class for itself," and gradually preparing the conditions for not only the abolition of capitalism ("total revolution") but also, *through their own initiative*, substituting "for the old civil society an association which will exclude classes and their antagonism."[21]

---

[19] Marx and Engels, *The German Ideology*, 52-53.
[20] As Geras aptly points out, the expression refers to, in part, "throwing off of all habits of deference acquired by virtue of its subordinate position in capitalist society and reinforced by the dominant ideology of that society." Geras, "Marxism and Proletarian Self-Emancipation," 21.
[21] Marx, *The Poverty of Philosophy*, 206-12.

Clearly, Marx was convinced that workers' combinations or associations were of crucial importance to the project of self-emancipation. He further proved his conviction by participating in their various activities, including delivering lectures on various topics. For instance, he had delivered several lectures on the issue of wages to the members of the German Workers' Society in Brussels in late 1847. The surviving manuscript, "Wages," contains a section on workers' associations. In it, Marx agrees with the claim of the "economists" that the costs of keeping these associations and using them to improve their wages are both economically unsound endeavors of the workers. (He would change his mind in this regard some years later.) Nevertheless, these associations are still very valuable, for "they are the means of uniting the working class, of preparing for the overthrow of the entire old society with its class contradictions." Interestingly, the only specific value Marx mentions here is that these associations "have the purpose of removing [competition among workers] and replacing it by union of workers."[22] If so, they are institutions of social dealienation, heralding the replacement of capitalism with a new form of society.

Another article, published in September 1847, reiterates the principle of self-emancipation, though this time against a fake "communist" (i.e., an agent-employee of the Prussian state), who published an article in which he claimed that "it is not the liberal bourgeoisie but the government which represents the interests of the proletariat."[23] According to Marx, such figures "delude themselves that the proletariat wishes to be helped, they do not conceive that it expects help from nobody but itself."[24] As noted in the previous chapter, he also argues in this article that the proletariat prefers (or ought to prefer) bourgeois democracy over "the rule of the bureaucracy" because the former would allow it to more freely utilize "the freedom of the press and the freedom of association" for the purpose of its self-emancipation.[25]

As crucially, Marx also reproaches the author of the article for preaching that "'a Christian state'" should not tolerate the misery of the proletariat. "The social principles of Christianity," Marx retorts,

[22] Marx, "Wages," 435.
[23] Marx, "The Communism of the *Rheinischer Beobachter*," 220.
[24] Ibid., 225.
[25] Ibid., 222, 225.

"preach cowardice, self-contempt, abasement, submissiveness and humbleness, in short, all the qualities of the rabble and the proletariat, which will not permit itself to be treated as rabble, needs its courage, its self-confidence, its pride and its sense of independence even more than its bread."[26] Here, the principle of self-emancipation is once more defended against the claim that the proletariat can/should be emancipated by others, including the state.

Marx and Engels highlight the importance of workers' combinations in the *Manifesto* (1848) as well, describing them as instruments of daily, localized class struggles. However, they stress, "The real fruit of their battles lies, not in the immediate result, but in the ever-expanding union of the workers." This movement is bringing about the "organization of the proletarians into a class, and consequently into a political party." Despite its rough trajectory of development, this organization helps overcome the "competition between the workers themselves," and has already compelled "legislative recognition of particular interests of the workers," such as "the ten-hours' bill in England."[27] Ultimately, this movement will lead to the final triumph of the proletariat and communism.

Marx and Engels believe that all this must be the work of the proletariat itself. Hence, they criticize the socialist utopians for seeing in the proletariat "a class without any historical initiative or any independent political movement." According to these universal "would-be reformers," social change "is to yield to their personal inventive action, historically created conditions of emancipation to fantastic ones, and the gradual, spontaneous class organization of the proletariat to an organization of society specially contrived by these inventors."[28] "The Communists" obviously defend the contrary view: The emancipation of the proletariat should be based on its own "initiative" and "spontaneous class organization."

There is, of course, a measure of irony in all this, for "the Communists," who are not themselves proletarians, write manifestos and programs on behalf of the proletariat. Still, it cannot be denied that Marx (and Engels) insisted on making the self-emancipation of the proletariat his own guiding principle. Although he never systematically explained why the proletariat cannot be

[26] Ibid., 231.
[27] Marx and Engels, *Manifesto of the Communist Party*, 493.
[28] Ibid., 515.

emancipated by others, the preceding analysis suggests strongly that the young Marx saw a crucial link between the practice of this principle and the emancipated society he envisioned. Through their organized struggles, workers would not only win important socialistic measures, such as the reduction of the working day, but also rid themselves "of all the muck of ages and become fitted to found society anew." Albeit in a somewhat scattered way, we have also seen that Marx thought workers' associations would serve as the media of dealienation. I will return to this issue in 7.4.

7.3 Self-Emancipation as the Principle of the International

Although he withdrew from "the game of making revolutions" in 1850s, Marx continued to study, and report in a journalistic fashion, the ongoing workers' struggles, especially the strikes in England, as well as the nexus between these struggles and workers' combinations. In the interest of brevity—otherwise we would be looking for needles in a haystack, I will mention only one of his reports, which was published in the *New York Daily Tribune* on July 14, 1853.

In it, Marx once again agrees with the claim, made by "a class of philanthropists, and even of socialists," that the struggles for the improvement of wages are bound to be frustrated. But, argues, the real value of these combinations consists in the fact that they are "the indispensable means of holding up the spirit of the laboring classes, of combining them into one great association against the encroachments of the ruling class, and of preventing them from becoming apathetic, thoughtless, more or less well-fed instruments of production." "In order to rightly appreciate the value of strikes and combinations," he adds, "we must" recognize that without them, "the working-classes of Great Britain, and of all Europe, would be a heart-broken, a weak-minded, a worn-out, unresisting mass, whose self-emancipation would prove as impossible as that of the slaves of Ancient Greece and Rome." Just as "the mediaeval communes" had been the "source of life of the now-ruling bourgeoisie," so would these combinations become the source of life of workers in the new society they would eventually create.[29]

---

[29] Marx, "Russian Policy Against Turkey and Chartism," 169.

The Principle of Self-Emancipation as Dealienation

Given his longstanding commitment to the self-emancipation of the working class via their combinations, it is not surprising at all that Marx also underscored the issue at hand in his "Inaugural Address of the International," which he completed drafting on October 27, 1864. It speaks favorably of the ongoing "co-operative movement," calling it the "victory of the political economy of labor over the political economy of property ..., especially the co-operative factories raised by the unassisted efforts of a few bold 'hands'."

> The value of these great social experiments cannot be over-rated. By deed, instead of by argument, they have shown that production on a large scale, and in accord with the behests of modern science, may be carried on without the existence of a class of masters employing a class of hands; that to bear fruit, the means of labor need not be monopolized as a means of dominion over, and of extortion against, the laboring man himself; and that, like slave labor, like serf labor, hired labor is but a transitory and inferior form, destined to disappear before associated labor plying its toil with a willing hand, a ready mind, and a joyous heart.[30]

Even a basic familiarity with the essential aspects of Marx's theory of alienation (see Chapter 2) should suffice to conclude that he regarded these "social experiments" as self-help experiments in dealienation, as this passage also illustrates. Overcoming alienation is thus the ethical ground of his support for them, even though he refrains from admitting the presence of such a ground in his support.

Yet, according to Marx, "however excellent in principle, and however useful in practice," these experiments "will never be able to ... free the masses, nor even to perceptibly lighten the burden of their miseries," unless they are "developed to national [general, society-level] dimensions, and, consequently, [are] fostered by national means."[31] In this context, Marx has in mind some sort of broader collectivization and democratic coordination of co-operative societies by workers themselves, though the terms of such

---

[30] Marx, "Inaugural Address of the Working Men's International Association," 11.
[31] Ibid., 12.

coordination are not specified. As we will see shortly, such "national means" cannot be state aid, assistance, or management, according to Marx, for these would reproduce dependence and servility.

Once again, the principle of self-emancipation grounds Marx's support for workers' cooperatives in the "Address." This is evinced by the fact that the preamble to the "Provisional Rules" of the International begins with it—and it is crucial that it begins with it: "That the emancipation of the working classes must be conquered by the working classes themselves; that the struggle for the emancipation of the working classes means not a struggle for class privileges and monopolies, but for equal rights and duties, and the abolition of all class rule."[32]

This statement also establishes a link between the self-emancipation of the working class and "the abolition of all class rule." The link basically underscores the *revolutionary* character of the principle and explains why Marx had frequently denounced, as merely reformist, those who did not include such expressions as this in their programs. The revolutionary character of the "Rules" is likewise enunciated in the third statement of the preamble: "That the economical emancipation of the working classes is ... the great end to which every political movement [of the workers' associations] ought to be subordinate as a means." Crucially, the second statement of the preamble defines "economical emancipation" as the abolition of "the economical subjection of the man of labor to the monopolizer of the means of labor, that is, the sources of life." This fundamental form of subjection, Marx writes with some sloganish exaggeration, "lies at the bottom of servitude in all its forms, of all social misery, mental degradation, and political dependence."[33] Once again, this is nothing less than the equation of self-emancipation with dealienation, a crucial vehicle of which is the development of workers' co-operative associations.

It is also crucial to note that the International was founded as an *international* association, echoing the famous slogan of the *Manifesto*: "Workingmen of all countries, unite!"[34] Relatedly, the

---

[32] Marx, "Provisional Rules of the Association," 14. As noted in Chapter 4, Marx reluctantly felt "obliged" to also include the expression "equal rights and duties."

[33] Ibid.

[34] Marx and Engels, *Manifesto of the Communist Party*, 519.

subsequent statements of the preamble warn against repeating the past mistakes, having to do with "the absence of a fraternal bond of union between the working classes of different countries," insisting that "the emancipation of labor is neither a local nor a national, but a social problem, embracing all countries in which modern society exists, and depending for its solution on the concurrence, practical and theoretical, of the most advanced countries." In short, "the present revival of the working classes in the most industrious countries of Europe, while it raises a new hope, gives solemn warning against a relapse into the old errors and calls for the immediate combination of the still disconnected movements." Moreover, this internationalism is to be guided by universalism, "without regard to color, creed, or nationality."[35] In short, a task of the International is to overcome the artificial fragmentation of humanity.

We get more details on the foregoing issues in the "Instructions for the Delegates of the Provisional General Council," penned by Marx and meant to frame the resolutions of the Geneva Congress of the International in 1866. Its highlights are the following: The main task of the International is "to combine and generalize the *spontaneous movements* of the working classes, but not to dictate or impose any doctrinaire system whatever. The Congress should, therefore, ... limit itself to the enunciation of a few general principles." Marx recommends the recognition of "the co-operative movement as one of the transforming forces of the present society based upon class antagonism." Why should this principle be promoted? Marx: "Its great merit is to practically show that the present pauperizing, and despotic system of *the subordination of labor* to capital can be superseded by the republican and beneficent system of *the association of free and equal producers*."[36] Therefore, the aim is to allow the working class to prove this to itself by its own deeds, and this in the manner of republican freedom (collective self-determination) and solidarism—two main antidotes to alienation.

Moreover, in order to realize the task of transforming capitalist society, the co-operative movement needs to eventually "convert social production into one large and harmonious system of free and

---

[35] Marx, "Provisional Rules of the Association," 14-15.
[36] Marx, "Instructions for the Delegates of the Provisional General Council. The Different Questions," 190.

co-operative labor." This will eventually require "the transfer of ... the state power from capitalists and landlords [and the bureaucrats] to the producers themselves," for the political rule of the working class will be ultimately needed to ensure the transformation of capitalist society (see Chapter 8). Via the International, Marx also recommends "to the working men to embark in *cooperative production* rather than [merely?] in *co-operative stores*," and "to all [existing] co-operative societies to convert one part of their joint income into a fund for propagating their principles by example as well as by precept, in other words, by promoting the establishment of new co-operative fabrics, as well as by teaching and preaching." In other words, the propagation of the co-operative societies is to be undertaken directly by workers themselves. Lastly, "In order to prevent co-operative societies from degenerating into ordinary middle-class joint stock companies, all workmen employed, whether shareholders or not, ought to share alike."[37]

The section of the "Instructions" on the issue of "Trades' Unions" is also very important. Against those who downplay their importance, including the Lassalleans in Germany, it declares their bread-and-butter struggles against capital "not only legitimate" but also "necessary," adding that these struggles "must be generalized by the formation and the combination of Trades' Unions throughout all countries." However, these unions "have not yet fully understood their power of acting against the system of wages slavery itself." To remedy this problem, they ought to also become "general social and political movements," which would render them "important *as organized agencies for superseding the very system of wages labor and capital rule*." They should also "enlist the non-society men into their ranks ..., look carefully after the interests of the worst paid trades, such as the agricultural laborers ..., and convince the world at large that their efforts, far from being narrow and selfish, aim at the emancipation of the downtrodden millions."[38]

---

[37] Ibid.
[38] Marx, "Instructions for the Delegates of the Provisional General Council," 191-92.

7.4 Self-Emancipation and Workers' Parties

In the meanwhile, Ferdinand Lassalle's supporters were following a different track in Germany from the one Marx had been at pains to formulate. In 1863, a year prior to his death, Lassalle founded the General Association of German Workers. By then, Marx had come to despise his former friend, Lassalle.[39] Politically and philosophically speaking, Marx was vehemently hostile to Lassalle's version of "socialism from above."[40] Thus, his February 18, 1865, letter to Engels warns that the Lassallean "party" in Germany "will discredit itself even more if it imagines that the Bismarck era or any other Prussian era will make the golden apples just drop into its mouth, by grace of the king," adding that "the working class is revolutionary or it is nothing." The letter also contains a statement, meant to be jointly submitted to the editors of the *Sozialdemokrat*, the organ of the Lassallean party. In it, the "undersigned" oppose "the royal Prussian governmental socialism."[41] The statement also mentions an earlier article (1847), in which, as quoted in the last section, Marx claims that the statists "delude themselves that the proletariat wishes to be helped; they do not conceive that it expects help from nobody but itself."[42]

To leap forward three years, to 1868, Marx was invited to attend the annual congress of the General Association of German Workers in Hamburg, to be held in August, as a guest of honor. The invitation was signed by Jean Baptista von Schweitzer, Lassalle's successor and the new president of the Association. The suspicious Marx interpreted Schweitzer's overture as an attempt to shore up his own credentials against the growing opposition to his Lassalleanism in the Association. In any case, as far as Marx was concerned, Schweitzer was committed to Lassalle's sectarian ways. Thus, although he is "greatly honored" by the invitation and regrets not being able to attend, Marx pointedly notes in his reply how he is

---

[39] For an account that links Marx's break with Lassalle to his hubris, see Rühle, *Karl Marx: His Life and Work*, 227-39.

[40] "The Structure of Lassalle's political thought was that of 'socialism from above,' by the grace of a Savior, and was therefore radically opposed to Marx's theory of the self-emancipatory revolution." Löwy, *The Theory of Revolution in the Young Marx*, 152.

[41] "Marx to Frederick Engels, February 18, 1865," 96.

[42] Marx, "The Communism of the *Rheinischer Beobachter*," 225.

happy to see that the program of [the Association's] Congress lays down those points from which, in fact, any serious workers' movement must proceed: agitation for complete political freedom, regulation [or reduction] of the working day, and systematic international cooperation of the working class in the great, historical task which it has to accomplish for the whole of society. Good luck in your work! With democratic greetings, Karl Marx.[43]

The intended swipe at Schweitzer, and Lassalleanism in general, in Marx's "democratic greetings" is obvious enough. Accordingly, with Schweitzer's overture in mind, his September 26, 1868, letter to Engels insists: "The most essential thing for the German working class is that it should cease to agitate by permission of the high government authorities. Such a bureaucratically schooled RACE [i.e. the Germans] must undergo a complete course of 'self-help'."[44] His next letter to Engels, written three days later, castigates Schweitzer for naively believing that "he can in a very simple way replace his dictatorship over the General Association of German Workers by the dictatorship over the German working class" as a whole. Marx concludes, wrongly as it would later turn out, that "Lassalleanism is already crumbling."[45]

How should he respond to Schweitzer? Engels: "I suggest you … find occasion to give Schweitzer a piece of your mind concerning his dictatorial ambitions, if you write to him at all."[46] His next letter to Marx follows up on this issue, noting how Schweitzer "has certainly been too cunning," especially in his efforts to impose handpicked presidents upon "the real workers' assemblies."[47] Marx's subsequent reply to Engels indicates his decision to "make it clear to [Schweitzer] that he must choose between the 'sect' [i.e., the dictatorial group imposing itself on the working class] and the 'class'."[48]

---

[43] Marx, "To the President and Executive Committee of the General Association of German Workers, August 18, 1868," 10.
[44] "Marx to Frederick Engels, September 26, 1868," 114-15
[45] "Marx to Frederick Engels, September 29, 1868," 116-17.
[46] "Engels to Karl Marx, September 30, 1868," 118.
[47] "Engels to Karl Marx, October 6, 1868," 125.
[48] "Marx to Frederick Engels, October 10, 1868," 127-28.

The Principle of Self-Emancipation as Dealienation

Marx at last replied to Schweitzer on October 13, with the aim to dispel Schweitzer's Lassallean "illusions." Thus, he first takes to task Lassalle's ideas and actions. On the issue of "state aid versus self-help," Lassalle had adopted the former in his day, and "was thus forced to make concessions to the Prussian monarchy, to Prussian reaction (the feudal party) and even to the clericals." Moreover, and relatedly, he founded a "doctrinaire ... sect," setting himself over and above the spontaneous workers' movement. Now, Marx maintains, Schweitzer himself is likewise demanding that "the class movement subordinate itself to a particular sect movement." Marx then takes a swipe at certain aspects of his "draft statutes," regarding the unions, claiming that Schweitzer's attempt to bring them under "a centralist organization ... contradicts the nature of the *trade unions.*" Marx reasons that this is an impossible aim and, even if it were possible, "it would not be desirable [anywhere], least of all in Germany." The importance of his explanation for this cannot be overemphasized: "[In Germany], where the worker is regulated bureaucratically from childhood onwards, where he believes in authority, in those set over him, the main thing is *to teach him to walk by himself.*"[49]

In all this we find an important secret of Marx's political philosophy: Self-emancipation is the antithesis of being "regulated bureaucratically." This explains the intended import of not only the cardinal principle of the International, "That the emancipation of the working classes must be conquered by the working classes themselves," but also the substantive "value" of workers' associations—social, economic, and political.

In 1875, Lassalle's followers and the "Eisenachers" (affiliated with Marx and Engels) came together to form the Socialist Workers' Party of Germany, which would become the Social Democratic Party of Germany in 1890. They drafted a program for the new party in Gotha—hence "the Gotha Program," which was sent to Marx for feedback. *Critique of the Gotha Program* is the title posthumously given to Marx's critique of it. The *Critique* contains many important themes, some of which will be considered in the next chapter. The ensuing paragraphs examine his castigation of the program's Lassallean appeal to state aid to help form workers' co-operatives.

---

[49] "Marx to Johann Baptist von Schweitzer, October 13, 1868," 132-35.

Marx's castigation is occasioned by the following demand made in the program:

> "The German Workers' party, in order *to pave the way to the solution of the social question*, demands the establishment of producers' co-operative societies *with state aid under the democratic control of the toiling people*. The producers' co-operative societies *are to be called into being* for industry and agriculture on such a scale *that the socialist organization of the total labor will arise from them*."[50]

The "*state aid*" aspect of the demand annoyed Marx immensely. Indeed, his visceral reaction to it comes across as unreasonable nitpicking. For instance, he engages in a wordplay to make the phrase "*the democratic control of the toiling people*'" appear more confused than it really is. He also complains, by way of vituperation, that in the Program, "'state aid' has been put 'under the democratic control of the working people'" purely out of "a sense of shame."[51]

In any case, if we leave aside Marx's exaggerated nitpicking, what remains from a philosophical standpoint is his hostility to the apparent *étatisme* of the Program, which he associates with Lassalle's "servile belief in the state."[52] Otherwise, Marx himself clearly endorses the demand to put such societies "under the democratic control of the working people."

Accordingly, Marx retorts that such societies should arise "from the revolutionary process of transformation of society," by which he means through the self-transforming activities of the German workers themselves. However, he seems to agree, without admitting to it, with the last part of the demand, as he, in his own wording, regards the desire of "the workers ... to establish the conditions for co-operative production on a social scale, and first of all on a national scale, in their own country [and later world-wide?]," as an attempt "to transform the present conditions of production." But, repeats Marx once more, this movement "has nothing in common with the foundation of co-operative societies with state aid."[53]

---

[50] Marx, *Critique of the Gotha Program*, 93.
[51] Ibid.
[52] Ibid., 97.
[53] Ibid., 93-94.

Delete the expression "state aid" and add the expressions "revolutionary" and "workers own activity" to it, and you get an agreement between Marx and the demand. Thus, such "co-operative societies," he adds in an already-familiar manner, "are of value only insofar as they are the independent creations of workers and not protégés either of the governments or of the bourgeoisie."[54]

Engels also circulated similar complaints about the "Gotha Program." One important thing he added to their common list of grievances—no doubt in agreement with Marx—was the need to give due importance to trade unions in the program. As his March 18-28, 1875, letter to Bebel insists, this "is a point of the utmost importance" since the trade unions are collectively "the proletariat's true class organization in which it fights its daily battles with capital, in which it trains itself."[55] The consistency of this passage with the principle of self-emancipation is obvious, especially since it comes at the heels of a paragraph in which Engels, like Marx, takes issue with the Lassallean appeal to state aid.

Alas, and this in passim, Marx's struggle against sectarianism went hand in hand, perhaps inescapably, with the development of his own sectarianism. This is evident, for instance, in his October 19, 1877, letter to Sorge:

> In Germany a corrupt spirit is asserting itself in our party, not much among the masses as among the leaders (upper class and [so-called] "workers"). The compromise with the Lassalleans has led to further compromise with other waverers; in Berlin (via [Johann] Most) with [Eugene] Dühring and his "admirers", not to mention a whole swarm of immature undergraduates and over-wise graduates who want to give socialism a "higher, idealistic" orientation, i.e. substitute for the materialist basis (which calls for serious, objective study if one is to operate thereon) a modern mythology with its goddesses of Justice, Liberty, Equality and *Fraternité*. Dr. [Karl] Höchberg ... is a representative of this tendency and has 'bought his way' into the party—no doubt with the "noblest" of intentions, but I don't give a fig for "intentions".[56]

---

[54] Ibid., 94.
[55] "Engels to August Bebel, March 18-28, 1875," 70.
[56] "Marx to Friedrich Adolph Sorge, October 19, 1877," 283.

As "our party" in Germany increased its membership and influence during the ensuing two years, arguably despite him, Marx had often found himself in the position of a naysayer. The Lassalleans, according to him, were incorrigible sectarians and state-worshipers. Johann Most, on the other hand, was guilty of "shouting for revolution by fire and sword,"[57] "silly secret conspiracy-mongering," and "plotting and scheming all over the place."[58] And, Höchberg (and co., including Eduard Bernstein) was a "a partisan of 'peaceable' ... emancipation of the proletariat ..., to be achieved solely by 'educated bourgeois', i.e. people like himself."[59] Moreover, "in the view of these gentlemen the Social-Democratic Party ought not to be a one-sided workers' party but a many-sided party of 'all men imbued with a true love of mankind'."[60] No wonder that Bebel, whom Marx and Engels trusted the most in Germany, later remarked: "It was no easy matter to arrive at an understanding with the two old men in London."[61]

Nevertheless, there was a remarkable consistency in Marx's fight against these and other fellows; in his view, they all rejected, one way or another, the principle of self-emancipation. It was about time to issue a threat. Should their own allies in Germany, such as Bebel, Wilhelm Bracke, and Wilhelm Liebknecht ("the Leipzigers"), continue to compromise with the rest, they "shall have to disavow them publicly," Marx tells Engels in his letter of September 10, 1879. "In such matters, the line has to be drawn somewhere."[62]

The line was drawn by Marx and Engels in what is known as the "Circular Letter," drafted on September 17-18, and sent to the Leipzigers. The letter goes through the many specific grievances enumerated above and concludes with the threat of withdrawing their "solidarity" with the party, unless they abandon their present course. More crucially, it sums up their political philosophy:

> For almost 40 years we have emphasized that the class struggle is the immediate motive force of history and, in particular, that the class struggle between bourgeoisie and proletariat is the

---

[57] "Marx to Carlo Cafiero," July 29, 1879, 365.
[58] "Marx to Friedrich Adolph Sorge, September 19, 1879," 411.
[59] Ibid., 413.
[60] Marx and Engels, "Circular Letter, September 17-18, 1879," 403.
[61] Quoted in McLellan, *Karl Marx*, 434.
[62] "Marx to Frederick Engels, September 10, 1879," 389.

great lever of modern social revolution; hence we cannot possibly co-operate with men who seek to eliminate that class struggle from the movement. At the founding of the International we expressly formulated the battle cry: The emancipation of the working class must be achieved by the working class itself. Hence, we cannot co-operate with men who say openly that the workers are too uneducated to emancipate themselves and must first be emancipated from above by philanthropic members of the upper and lower middle classes.[63]

As noted in the previous chapter, about a year later, Marx and Engels found themselves entangled in the affairs of another party. Clearly to their delight, Jules Guesde and Paul Lafargue (Marx's son-in-law) met with them at Marx's residence to collectively write the program of the newly-formed *Parti Ouvrier*; its most substantial parts were written by Marx himself.[64] Importantly, in some measure, it was written against the revolutionary-conspiratorial tendencies in France. Thus, in his November 5, 1880, letter to Sorge, Marx describes the program as a successful articulation of "the communist aim … in a few lines," adding that its relatively modest, realistic demands represent "a tremendous step forward" in terms of bringing "the French workers down to earth out of their verbal cloud-cuckoo land." For this reason, and unsurprisingly, the program has "aroused much resentment among all those French intellectual frauds who make a living as 'cloud-assemblers'." Marx further stresses in his letter to Sorge that the French party "nevertheless adopted most of the 'practical' demands in the program," thus proving to be "*the first real workers' movement* in France."[65]

In a sense, too, the "The Program of the *Parti Ouvrier*" tells us much about the kind of program Marx and Engels wanted his German comrades to adopt also. Its preamble displays its four main principles. First, "the emancipation of the productive class is that of all human beings without distinction of sex or race." Second, its emancipation requires collective "possession of the means of production." Third, and hence the principle of self-emancipation, "this collective appropriation can arise only from the revolutionary

[63] Marx and Engels, "Circular Letter, September 17-18, 1879," 408.
[64] For a first-hand account of its composition, see "Engels to Eduard Bernstein, October 25, 1881," 148-49.
[65] "Marx to Friedrich Adolph Sorge, November 5, 1880, 44."

action of the productive class—or proletariat organized in a distinct political party." Fourth, "such an organization must be pursued by all the means the proletariat has at its disposal including universal suffrage which will thus be transformed from the instrument of deception that it has been until now into an instrument of emancipation." The immediate aim of the party is "to enter the elections" with France-specific "political" and "economic" demands, which can be non-controversially deemed by us as modest social-democratic demands.[66]

7.5 "Sprouts" of Communism

The principle of self-emancipation and one of its key vehicles, namely, workers' co-operatives, also appears in the third volume of *Capital*. According to Shlomo Avineri, Marx here "tries to relate the theory propounded here to his theory of alienation. The separation of ownership from control and management must also be viewed as the climax of alienation. Not only is the worker alienated from his labor; even the capitalist is alienated, in the more sophisticated form of capitalist society, from his capital."[67]

Marx thus goes on to conclude that

> In stock companies the function is divorced from capital ownership, hence also labor is entirely divorced from ownership of means of production and surplus labor. This result of the ultimate development of capitalist production is a necessary transitional phase towards the reconversion of capital into the property of producers, although no longer as the private property of the individual producers, but rather as the property of associated producers, as direct social property.[68]

The same is likewise true of "the co-operative factories of the laborers themselves," Marx further argues, adding that they too "represent within the old form [i.e., within capitalism] the first sprouts of the new [society, namely, communism]," despite—for the reasons we have discussed in the preceding section—their "shortcomings." The aspect Marx singles out here to explain why

---

[66] www.marxists.org/archive/marx/works/1880/05/parti-ouvrier.htm

[67] Avineri, *The Social and Political Thought of Karl Marx*, 177-78.

[68] Karl Marx, *Capital*, Vol. 3, 434.

the "co-operative factories of the laborers" are such "sprouts" is very significant: "The antithesis between capital and labor is overcome within them." This is assumed to be nothing other than a significant step in the negation of alienation. It is, positively put, an important step toward achieving *freedom* (dealienation) within the sphere of production, thus radically altering the structure of bourgeois society.

Clearly, workers' co-operatives, as Marx conceives them, are transitional remedies for the aspects of alienation he articulates in this context. In his wording, "The capitalist stock companies, as much as the co-operative factories, should be considered as transitional forms from the capitalist mode of production to the associated one, with the only distinction that the antagonism is resolved negatively in the one and positively in the other." This also shows how "a new mode of production naturally grows out of an old one."[69] The transition to communism (i.e., the gradual revolution) thus begins (or ought to begin) in capitalism, according to Marx, and this with the development of the "sprouts" of the future society.

Three years later, in 1871, Marx defended similar ideas, which were occasioned by the Paris Commune. "The Commune," maintains he approvingly in *The Civil War in France*, "intended to abolish that class-property which makes the labor of the many the wealth of the few. It aimed at the expropriation of the expropriators. It wanted to make individual property a truth by transforming the means of production, land and capital, now chiefly the means of enslaving and exploiting labor, into mere instruments of free and associated labor." By "free and associated labor," he means collectively owned and managed co-operatives. However, there is an important and familiar proviso:

> If co-operative production is not to remain a sham and a snare; if it is to supersede the Capitalist system; if united co-operative societies are to regulate national production upon a common plan, thus taking it under their own control, and putting an end to the constant anarchy and periodical convulsions which are the fatality of Capitalist production—what else, gentlemen, would it be but Communism, 'possible' Communism?[70]

---

[69] Ibid., 438.
[70] Marx, *The Civil War in France*, 335.

Here, I argue, Marx has in mind a scheme of economic coordination and regulation ("centralization") that parallels the proposed bottom-up, expansively-democratic political structure of the Commune—direct local self-governments feeding into regional and national system of representation and accountable administration (see Chapter 8).

The "late" Marx's comments on Russia are also of interest to our present inquiry. An adequate commentary on these comments and their context falls beyond the scope of this section.[71] However, a few relevant comments are in order.

The most well-known of such comments appear in Marx's letters to the editorial board of the *Otechestvenniye Zapiski* (1877) and to Vera Zasulich (1881). The latter letter was posted to its addressee, but not the former. There also exist four drafts of the succinct letter to Zasulich, two of which are quite lengthy. The key question Marx attempts to answer in both letters and the drafts is whether the Russian commune system could be the foundation of socialism, allowing Russia to leap over the stages of capitalist development.

In his letter to the *Otechestvenniye Zapiski*, and despite the evidence to the contrary, Marx denies the charges that he, in *Capital*, defends the "historico-philosophical theory of general development, imposed by fate on all peoples." He also argues that Russia "can acquire all the fruits of this [commune] system without suffering … [all the] torments [of capitalist development]." In short, "if Russia continues along the road [of building capitalism at the expense of the communes,] which it has followed since 1861, it will forego the finest opportunity that history has ever placed before a nation, and will undergo all the fateful misfortune of capitalist development."[72]

In his letter to Zasulich, Marx (based on the revisions he had already made to the French edition) argues mischievously that he "*expressly*" limits the stages-theory "to the *countries of Western Europe*" in *Capital*. "Hence the analysis provided in *Capital* does not adduce reasons either for or against the viability of the rural commune." More crucially for our present purposes, he is

---

[71] For an excellent analysis of Marx's approach to the question of Russia, see Wada, "Marx and Revolutionary Russia." Some of the claims I make below are amply demonstrated in Wada's piece.

[72] "Marx to *Otechestvenniye Zapiski*, November 1877," 199.

"convinced" that "this commune is the fulcrum of social regeneration in Russia," provided that its "normal conditions of spontaneous development" are not thwarted by the state, the bourgeoisie, and the emergent class of *kulaks*.[73]

Unfortunately, Marx's comments on Russia have been reduced by his followers to the issue of the possibility of a successful communist revolution (putsch) in economically underdeveloped countries, such as Russia.[74] For Marx, however, the central question was whether the Russian commune system could be effectively turned into "the fulcrum of social regeneration in Russia," which implies a different kind of revolution. Thus, in the lengthy "First Draft" of the letter to Zasulich, Marx speaks of the need to supply the communes with technology and, as importantly, to bring them into a coordinated unity. In other words, if correctly handled and safeguarded against the existing threats to it, the commune-system "can become a direct point of departure for the economic system [i.e., communism] towards which modern society tends." There is also a political-democratic requirement: "It would ... be necessary to replace the *volost*, the [regional] government body, with an assembly of peasants elected by the communes themselves, serving as the economic and administrative organ for their interests." However, given its current trajectory, the commune, this potential sprout of the future society, is bound to disappear, *unless* a revolution in Russia helps rejuvenate it.[75]

***

Although he in nowise had ever abandoned the desideratum of a communist revolution, and on occasion wishfully thought it might breakout somewhere soon, Marx had no specific plan to urge one to occur after 1850. This claim, of course, is true only if by

---

[73] "Marx to Vera Zasulich, March 8, 1881," 370-71.

[74] As Hudis correctly points out, even though Marx "entertained the possibility that a [socially and technologically underdeveloped] country like Russia could experience a socialist *revolution* ahead of the West, he held that it would not succeed [in *establishing* socialism] unless the revolution was joined and supported by a proletarian revolution in the industrially-developed countries. Hudis, *Marx's Concept of the Alterative to Communism*, 210 n. 7.

[75] "Marx to Vera Zasulich (First Draft), March 3, 1881," 353-54.

"revolution" we mean an *insurrection* during which workers were to seize political power rather rapidly. However, the findings of this chapter suggest very strongly that he had, until his final hours, enjoined another kind of revolution—the kind that he thought was already occurring in a "protracted" manner through the organized political and economic struggles of the working class—and perhaps the peasants in some places. From this vantage point, the transition to socialism had already began, consistently with his dictum that "a new mode of production naturally grows out of an old one."[76]

This transition could be observed in the development of the "sprouts" of the future society, such as workers' co-operative societies, labor unions, and the like, not to forget the possibilities offered by the Russian communes in that country. Of course, although in some sense inevitable (see Chapter 5), Marx thought it was necessary to wage coordinated struggles to foster the development of these "sprouts." Crucially, it was also necessary to urge the proletariat to form independent political parties, with the aim of eventually seizing political power. At this point, I suppose, a society could be properly called "socialist" or "communist." To clarify, Marx thought this would constitute only a significant turning point in the transition to a full-blown socialist society—neither its beginning nor consummation (see Chapter 8).

All this must be based on the principle of self-emancipation, Marx had insisted all along. As this chapter sufficiently illustrated, and as Engels' "Preface" to the 1888 English edition of the *Manifesto* confirms, he and Marx had defended this principle "from the very beginning."[77] The intrinsic "value" of the "sprouts" lies in the fact that they are the proper media of self-emancipation, which essentially means self-dealienation. This is the specific sense in which the present chapter has demonstrated the veracity of Michael Löwy's claim: In Marx's view, alienation can be overcome "only in a non-alienated way: the character of the new society is determined by the very process of its creation."[78] It should thus come as no surprise to learn that Marx's vision of communism dovetails this very idea, as the next chapter illustrates.

---

[76] Marx, *Capital*, Vol. 3, 438.
[77] Engels, "Preface to the 1888 English Edition of *Manifesto of The Communist Party*," 517.
[78] Löwy, *The Theory of Revolution in the Young Marx*, 112.

Communism: The Realm of Freedom

8.1 Introduction

To borrow Steven Lukes' expression, Marx was anti-utopian utopian.[1] As the former, he not only disparaged utopianism but also denied having ever himself imagined a communist system.[2] If so, a positive vision of socialism or communism[3] cannot be attributed to the anti-utopian Marx. However, despite himself, he imagined an ideal future society, communism, and so was a utopian thinker for this reason. I believe his utopianism and anti-utopianism cannot be reconciled. Since the main aim of this chapter is to reconstruct his vision of communism, his anti-utopianism will be bracketed out.

However, his anti-utopian stance cannot be entirely ignored, even when the aim is to reconstruct his utopia. For one thing, as 8.2 illustrates, Marx defined himself as an anti-utopian critical scientist. So, it behooves us to understand and explore this fact in a chapter on his idea of communism. For another, his anti-utopianism explains the sketchy nature of his vision of communism. In other words, the ensuing reconstruction of this vision will necessarily be choppy. Nevertheless, an attractive eudemonistic image of a good life will emerge from it.

The dictatorship of the proletariat is the first crucial feature of Marx's utopia this chapter considers. The utopian aspect of this dictatorship mainly consists in its institutional form (expansive democracy) and aim to achieve freedom in a classless society (8.3).

---

[1] Lukes, "Marxism and Utopianism," 155. For informative surveys of various interpretations of the Marx-utopianism nexus, including their own interesting takes on it, see Webb, *Marx, Marxism, and Utopia*; Paden, "Marx's Critique of the Utopian Socialists"; Geoghegan, *Utopianism and Marxism*.

[2] At least on one occasion, Marx defined utopianism as "the play of the imagination on the future structure of [the good] society." "Marx to Friedrich Adolph Sorge, October 19, 1877," 284. I use this definition, adding that utopianism imagines a desirable, "good" society; it does not necessarily imagine an impractical scheme of things.

[3] The popular claim that Marx regarded socialism as the lower or initial stage of communism is a later invention. In truth, he used these two terms interchangeably. See Chattopadhyay, *Socialism and Commodity Production*, Ch. 1.

Based on the material presented in Chapter 7, I take it for granted in this chapter that collective ownership and democratic control of the means of production are also fundamental features of Marx's utopia. How is the collectively produced wealth to be distributed in socialism? As 8.4 illustrates, Marx considered two communistic principles of distribution: equal renumeration for equal hours of work and to each according to his/her needs. It will be seen that he preferred the latter principle from a humanist-ethical standpoint, despite his materialist pretentions to the contrary.

However, Marx was less interested in the principles of distribution than he was in the principle of freedom. He regarded maximizing both free, disposable time and all-round activity as essential to human self-realization, defined as self-development or flourishing. Relatedly, he defined communism as the positive transcendence (abolition or sublation) of alienation, and so envisioned it as the realization of human essence in existence (8.5). The chapter concludes by stressing that this latter point is the crux of Marx's humanist practical-revolutionary philosophy of freedom. This is also the conclusion of the present study.

8.2 Anti-Utopianism

An early example of Marx's opposition to utopianism is found in his September 1843 letter to Arnold Ruge, especially in the following lines: "But, if constructing the future and settling everything for all times are not our affair, it is all the more clear what we have to accomplish at present: I am referring to *ruthless criticism of all that exists* ... Therefore, I am not in favor of raising any dogmatic banner." However, before reaching this conclusion, he also expresses his wish to "find the new world through criticism of the old one."[4] This renders his anti-utopianism ambivalent.

In *The German Ideology*, we read: "Communism is for us not a state of affairs which is to be established, an *ideal* to which *reality* [will] have to adjust itself. We call communism the real movement which abolishes the present state of things."[5] It seems that Marx's

---

[4] "Marx to Arnold Ruge, September 1843," 142.

[5] Marx and Engels, *The German Ideology*, 49. Marx and Engels also claim to derive their idea of communism "from examining the real state of affairs." In this, they are distinguished from the so-called "'true socialists',," who derive theirs "by a process of 'pure thought'" (ibid., 455).

own *"ruthless criticism of all that exists"* has now become "the real movement which abolishes the present state of things." In any case, this popular passage unhelpfully renders the concept of communism meaningless. To further compound the problem, it is not entirely clear to what this negative "movement" refers. Also, this text contains images of, to wit, "an *ideal* to which *reality* [will] have to adjust itself," as we shall see in 8.5. In short, the anti-utopianism of this text is likewise ambivalent. However, its authors clearly do not regard themselves as utopians, which, perhaps, explains why such images in the text are scarce.

The *Manifesto* is likewise ambivalent on this issue, and in very similar ways. It disparages the "true socialists" for their philosophical idealism, and takes to task, among a host of other socialist schools, the critical-utopian socialists. However, the latter are treated more favorably, especially since they "attack every principle of existing society." Thus, Marx and Engels value the "critical element" in their thinking, but not their diagnoses of social problems and their means to overcome them. Moreover, they unequivocally denounce the utopians' images of the future society as "castles in the air,"[6] but do not refrain from imagining a few key features of the future society they themselves prefer. In the final analysis, though, they appear to regard themselves as anti-utopian materialists.

"If a roundabout story is credible ..., Georges Sorel in the *Réflexions sur la violence* (1908) reported that, according to the economist Professor Lujo Brentano, Marx wrote the English Positivist Edward Spencer Beesly in 1869: 'The man who draws up a program for the future is a reactionary.'"[7] If this "roundabout story" does not put to rest Marx's previous ambiguities with respect to his critique of the utopian socialists, his first draft of *The Civil War in France* (1871) does:

> The Utopian founders of sects, while in their criticism of present society clearly describe the goal of the social movement, [which is] the supersession of the wages system with all its economic conditions of class rule, found neither in society itself the material conditions of its transformation nor

---

[6] Marx and Engels, *Manifesto of the Communist Party*, 515-16.
[7] Manuel and Manuel, *Utopian Thought in the Western World*, 698.

in the working class the organized power and the conscience of the movement. They tried to compensate for the historical conditions of the movement by fantastic pictures and plans of a new society in whose propaganda they saw the true means of salvation. From the moment the workingmen class movement became real, the fantastic Utopias evanesced, *not because the working class had given up the end aimed at by these Utopists, but because they had found the real means to realize them* [emphasis added].[8]

This somewhat ambiguous passage is frequently misunderstood. If read carefully, however, Marx only agrees with the *negative* aim of the socialist utopians, viz., to *abolish* or *suppress* "the wages system with all its economic conditions of class rule." He does not agree with either their means or *positive* ends, which are but "fantastic Utopias." Thus, as Darren Webb aptly puts it,

What Marx is saying here is *not* that the working class had found the appropriate means of realizing the Utopians' utopias, but rather that they had found the appropriate means of realizing the [negative] goal *aimed at* by the Utopians, which was the suppression of the wages system.[9]

If correctly understood in this way, Marx's comment on utopianism in the final version of *The Civil War in France* repeats the criticism of the same in its first draft, contrary to the claims that it departs from it. It reads: "The working class [i.e. Marx] ... have no ready-made Utopias to introduce *par décret du people* ... They have no ideals to realize, but to set free elements of the new society with which old collapsing bourgeois society itself is pregnant."[10]

Marx also consistently denied being a utopian craftsman of the future society. His pertinent comment in the "Afterword" to the second German edition of *Capital* (1872) is a case in point. He claims there that in his review of *Capital*, Eugène de Roberty, a

---

[8] Marx, "First Draft of *The Civil War in France*," 499-500.

[9] Webb, *Marx, Marxism, and Utopia*, 29. Therefore, it is not true that Marx simply criticized "the inadequacy of the means" of "the utopian socialists," but shared their positive "ends." *Pace* Meisner, *Marxism, Maoism, and Utopianism*, 8.

[10] Karl Marx, *The Civil War in France*, 335.

follower of Auguste Comte, the famed positivist, criticizes him for 1) treating "economics metaphysically" and 2) confining himself "to the mere critical analysis of actual facts, instead of writing receipts [or recipes] (Comtist ones?) for the cook-shops of the future."[11] What Marx does not mention is that these two criticisms issue from de Roberty's 1) hope to see in the subsequent volumes of *Capital* "less dialectic and even greater use of the inductive method, if that is possible," without which, 2) in the subsequent volumes of *Capital*, Marx will not be able to investigate "the *necessary conditions* for healthy production and a just distribution of wealth."[12] This latter criticism is informed by what de Roberty takes to be, and for good reasons, Marx's ready-made dialectical-materialist induction of communistic appropriation of the means of consumption in the first volume of *Capital*. Thus, he expects and urges a better justification for socialism, and not a laundry-list of Comtist recipes *per se*. In any case, Marx quickly and sarcastically accepts the unmade charge.

However, Marx's focus here is on de Roberty's first criticism. This is so because he mentions the latter's review right after complaining that "the method employed in 'Das Kapital' has been little understood."[13] Subsequently, he quotes a "Russian" reviewer, who claims that "the scientific value" of Marx's "'inquiry lies in the disclosing of the special laws that regulate the origin, existence, development, death of a given social organism and its replacement by another and higher one.'" The "writer," Marx remarks approvingly, here unwittingly describes the crux of his, Marx's, scientific-*materialist* "dialectic method."[14] By extension, Marx accepts predicting the inevitable replacement of capitalism by communism with his (eminently unscientific) materialistic version

---

[11] Karl Marx, *Capital*, Vol. 1, 17.

[12] The review is reproduced in Marx, *Capital: A Critical Analysis of Capitalist Production, London 1887*, 783.

[13] Marx, *Capital*, Vol. 1, 17.

[14] Ibid., 19. This is where Marx claims to turn Hegel's idealist dialectic right-side-up. In part, this is a response to Eugen Dühring's disparagement of his "nonsensical" Hegelian dialectic (see the next footnote). In a letter to Kugelmann, Marx opines that Dühring "knows full well that my method of exposition is *not* Hegelian, since I am a materialist, and Hegel an idealist." "Marx to Ludwig Kugelmann, March 6, 1868," 544.

of the infamous Hegelian dialectical formula of the negation of the negation.[15] In short, this is *all* he seems to admit doing: He merely predicts, "scientifically" he would have us believe, the inevitable demise of capitalism and the arrival of communism.

To return to the Commune, Marx regarded its expansively democratic institutions as the model for the future society (see 8.3). This issue came up in his conspectus on Bakunin's *Statehood and Anarchy*, in which Marx claims to have previously used the expression "*scientific socialism* ... only in contrast to Utopian socialism, which wishes to foist new illusions onto the people instead of confining its scientific investigations to the social movement created by the people itself."[16] Thus, he once more claims to base his vision of socialism strictly on what "the people" have *already* created. By extension, this means that "Utopian socialism" consists of unscientific illusions, on account of not basing its socialist ideas on the creations of "the people," by which he means the working class. The claim lends itself to the strange conclusion that socialism is simply what workers create.

Alas, in his October 19, 1877, letter to Sorge, Marx remarkably belittles the theoretical capacities of workers—the last thing one would expect from the workerist philosopher of self-emancipation. "The workers ..., when like Mr. [Johann] Most and Co. ..., give up working and become *literati by profession*," he opines, "invariably wreak 'theoretical' havoc and are always ready to consort with addle-heads of the supposedly 'learned' caste." More specifically, they refuse to accept Marx's science. They thus undermine what he "had been at such pains to eject from the German workers' heads," namely, *utopianism*, which he defines, more clearly than ever before, as "the play of the imagination on the future structure of

---

[15] In fact, this "dialectical prediction on the advent of communism had been repeatedly made years before he wrote *Capital*." Horie, *Marx's Capital and One Free World*, 112. The one in *Capital*, Vol. 1 occurs in pages 750-51. According to Eugen Dühring, "It would be difficult to convince a sensible man of the necessity of ... [communism] on the basis of credence in Hegelian word-juggling such as the negation of the negation." Quoted in Engels, *Anti-Dühring: Herr Eugen Dühring's Revolution in Science*, 120. Engel's book is devoted to defending Marx's dialectic against Dühring.

[16] Marx, "Notes on Bakunin's Book *Statehood and Anarchy*," 520.

society." He then plays the already-familiar tune: "Utopianism which bore within itself the seeds of critical and materialist socialism, before the advent of the latter, can now, post festum, only seem silly, stale and thoroughly reactionary."[17] In short, Marx's "critical and materialist socialism" is not utopian because it does not entail "imagination on the future structure of society." It is, in the main, critical and merely heralds the inevitable arrival of that society. All else is reactionary.

Marx reaches this conclusion unambiguously in his letter to Nieuwenhuis, written on February 22, 1881. He argues in it that any vision of the future society is necessarily undesirable, if not reactionary. Consistently with his gradualism, he first warns against premature revolutions—with the experience of the Commune in mind—and then argues that the shape of the future society cannot be anticipated. In fact, he assures "comrade" Nieuwenhuis, "a doctrinaire and of necessity [!] fantastic anticipation of a future revolution's program of action only serves to distract from the present struggle." But he should rest assured that

> Scientific insight into the inevitable disintegration, now steadily taking place before our eyes, of the prevailing social order; the masses themselves, their fury mounting under the lash of the old governmental bogies; the gigantic and positive advances simultaneously taking place in the development of the means of production—all this is sufficient guarantee that the moment a truly proletarian revolution breaks out, the conditions for its immediate initial (if certainly not idyllic) *modus operandi* will also be there.[18]

A few months later, Marx penned down extensive notes on Adolph Wagner's *Lehrbuch der politischen Ökonomie*, which criticizes Marx's economic theories. What concern us here are their comments on socialism. Wagner: "Marx's theory of value is the 'cornerstone of his socialist system'." Marx: "As I have never established a 'socialist system', this is a fantasy of Wagner, [Albert] Schäffle, *e tutti quanti*." Wagner: "'Not only does [Marx's theory of value] not correspond to the *formation of exchange-value* in *present-*

---

[17] "Marx to Friedrich Adolph Sorge, October 19, 1877," 283-84.
[18] "Marx to Ferdinand Domela Nieuwenhuis, February 22, 1881," 66-67.

day commerce …, but neither, as *Schäffle* excellently and indeed conclusively demonstrates in the *Quintessenz* and especially in the *Socialer Körper*, does it correspond to conditions as they are bound to take shape in the Marxian hypothetical social state'." Marx: "That is the social state, which Mr. Schäffle was courteous enough to 'shape' for me, is transformed into 'the Marxian' (not the 'social state' foisted on to Marx in Schäffle's hypothesis)." Marx again: "In my *investigation of value*, I have dealt with bourgeois relations [only], not with the application of this theory of *value* to a 'social state' …, constructed by … Mr. Schäffle for me."[19]

Did "Mr. Schäffle" invent Marx's "social state"? In his *The Quintessence of Socialism*, he acknowledges that "The leaders of the international movement, especially Karl Marx, in his bitingly critical and undeniably clear-sighted work 'Das Kapital,' are, it is true, very cautious in enunciating their positive program."[20] Schäffle goes on to admire Marx's "extreme caution" in this regard, noting accurately that "the principal requirement" for the likes of Marx presently "is negative criticism of the existing state of things." Still, these socialists offer a positive vision of socialism, and the "*resumé* which Karl Marx gives at the end of his critique on capital is in every respect the most definite and significant statement we have." He then goes on to generously quote form the first volume of *Capital* to outline this most significant *resumé* of socialism.[21] Later, he praises Marx's theory of exploitation, and then illustrates how he envisions a socialist society based on collective ownership of the means of production and a nonexploitative scheme of distribution.[22] He derives this material from a section of *Capital*, which begins with these words: "Let us now picture to ourselves … a community of free individuals …," which he also calls "our imagined association."[23]

At the end of his book, Schäffle summarizes the conclusion of his indictment of Marx's *magnum opus*:

[19] Marx, "Notes on Wagner's *Lehrbuch der politischen Oekonomie,*" 533, 536, 537.
[20] Schäffle, *The Quintessence of Socialism*, 6.
[21] Ibid., 11-17. See Marx, *Capital*, Vol. 1, 748-51.
[22] Schäffle, *The Quintessence of Socialism*, 24-31.
[23] Marx, *Capital*, Vol. 1, 89ff.

It has been proved ... that Marx's theory of democratic collectivism—the social democracy—represents an impracticable program, which leads down to economic chaos; for till now, this democratic socialism has retained as its basis Marx's theory of value as depending on social labor-cost.[24]

If so, while the merits of Schäffle's "proof" are debatable, the fact that he copied Marx's "hypothetical social state" from *Capital* is not. "Marx had been correctly reported by Schäffle."[25]

Marx's proven familiarity with Schäffle's *Die Quintessenz des Socialismus* makes his contrary claim all-the-more remarkable. On a related note, he ridicules this book in a private correspondence for being an "unintentional comedy," not least because "Mr. Schäffle, with a fantasy truly Swabian [meant as an insult], paints so pretty a picture of the future socialist millennium as to make it seem the kingdom come of your cozy petty bourgeois."[26] To be sure, Marx's vituperation is not simply a critique of Schäffle's version of "the future socialist millennium." Rather, it is consistent with his longstanding, wholesale condemnation of *all* such visions.

The present section has illustrated Marx's longstanding anti-utopianism and, which is essentially the same thing, denial of envisioning a utopia of his own. The ensuing sections will illustrate his utopianism. I do not think these contradictory positions, what Lukes calls a "sub-paradox" within Marx's anti-morality moralism,[27] could be reconciled on evidentiary basis. Thus, I will henceforth bracket out his anti-utopianism.

8.3 Democratic Dictatorship of the Proletariat

In *The Poverty of Philosophy*, Marx asks: "Does ... [it] mean that after the fall of the old society there will be a new class domination culminating in a new political power?" His answer is simply "No." It is based on the questionable assumption that "political power" and "class domination" are synonymous terms, meaning that communism will not entail political power because it

---

[24] Schäffle, *The Quintessence of Socialism*, 120.

[25] Moore, *Marx on the Choice between Socialism and Communism*, 89.

[26] "Marx to Ferdinand Feckles, January 21, 1877," 190.

[27] Lukes, *Marxism and Morality*, 37.

will be a classless society.[28] In any case, given that it is not a factual answer, we would be apt to regard it as a desideratum, an advocacy for not only "the abolition of all classes" but also substituting "for the old civil society an association [a communist society] which will exclude classes and their antagonism."[29]

This very idea is also repeated in the "anti-utopian" *Manifesto*: "If the proletariat ... by means of a revolution ... makes itself the ruling class ..., then it will [after a protracted transitional period] ... have swept away the conditions for the existence of class antagonisms and of classes generally, and will thereby have abolished its own supremacy as a class." Consequently, "we shall have an association, in which the free development of each is the condition for the free development of all."[30] So, Marx once again appears to have a utopian vision of the future, despite his curious manner of expressing it—as if it were a scientific prediction.

However, the *Manifesto* suggests a statist model for the proletarian rule: "The proletariat will use its political supremacy to [gradually] wrest, by degrees, all capital from the bourgeoisie, to centralize all instruments of production in the hands of the State, i.e., of the proletariat organized as the ruling class." The ten transitional measures Marx and Engels propose, to be implemented after the proletariat seizes political power, also smack of *étatisme* as several of them directly feed into the general aim to centralize "all instruments of production in the hands of the State."[31]

That this is to emerge after the proletariat becomes the ruling class by winning "the battle of democracy" does little to erase the *étatisme* of the *Manifesto*. However, its reference to communism as "an association, in which the free development of each is the condition for the free development of all," implies that the state will be necessary only during the initial stages of communism. This means that the *Manifesto* imagines the future society in transitional terms. Marx (and Engels) would continue to think of it in this way until the end of his life. However, he would soon abandon the temporally limited *étatisme* of the *Manifesto*.

This *étatisme* was recently acquired and would soon become

---

[28] As we have seen in Chapter 3 and will further see in this chapter, he also acknowledges the state bureaucracy as such as a power in some of his writings.

[29] Marx, *The Poverty of Philosophy*, 212.

[30] Marx and Engels, *Manifesto of the Communist Party*, 504.

[31] Ibid, 505.

even acuter—tellingly, during the period in which Marx and Engels collaborated with the Blanquists in the Communist League. Indeed, if not already in 1848, Marx and Engels defended a top-down dictatorship during this period. This is clearly visible in their March 1850 "Address of the Central Authority to the League."[32]

To summarize, "The workers," the "Address" declares, "must not only strive for a single and indivisible German republic, but also within this republic for the most determined centralization of power in the hands of the state authority." Relatedly, the German workers "must not allow themselves to be misguided by the democratic talk of freedom for the communities, of self-government, etc. ... [I]t is the task of the really revolutionary party to carry through the strictest centralization." In addition, the aim should be "to concentrate the utmost possible productive forces, means of transport, factories, railways, etc., in the hands of the state."[33]

In the meanwhile, Marx began referring to the political supremacy of the proletariat as *the dictatorship of the proletariat*, and this in *The Class Struggles in France* (1850—originally written as a set of articles, published in the *Neue Rheinische Zeitung*).[34] Variously worded versions of the expression appear thrice in this text, the most significant of which refers to "the *class dictatorship* of the proletariat as the necessary transit point to the *abolition of class distinctions generally*, to the abolition of all the relations of production on which they rest, to the abolition of all the social relations that correspond to these relations of production, to the revolutionizing of all the ideas that result from these social relations."[35] Another reference to it suggests that "the revolutionary dictatorship" of the proletariat should be led by the working class, not by a "sectarian" sect of leaders.[36]

In his letter of March 5, 1852, to Weydemeyer, Marx claims to have contributed (or discovered) the following triadic view: "1. ...

---

[32] Marx and Engels, "Address of the Central Authority to the League," 285-86.

[33] Ibid., 86.

[34] For an almost exhaustive treatment of the origin and uses of this concept, see Draper, *Karl Marx's Theory of Revolution, The "Dictatorship of the Proletariat,"* 34-39, 111-71.

[35] Marx, *The Class Struggles in France, 1848 to 1850*, 127.

[36] Ibid., 98.

that the *existence of classes* is merely bound up with *certain historical phases in the development of production*; 2. that the class struggle necessarily leads to the *dictatorship of the proletariat*; 3. that this dictatorship itself constitutes no more than a transition to the *abolition of all classes* and to a *classless society.*"[37] What makes this letter of additional interest for our present purposes is its date.

At about the same time Marx completed his *The Eighteenth Brumaire*. This coincidence of the dates suggests strongly that he now thought the dictatorship of the proletariat should not be a bureaucratic state, the antithesis of self-government. In this text, and in a way reminiscent of his 1843 critique of Hegel's philosophy of the state, Marx identifies the modern—specifically the French—state with its executive power. This entity, he laments, "possesses an immense bureaucratic and military organization, with its extensive and artificial state machinery ..., which enmeshes the body of French society like a net and chokes all its pores." He then predicts that the next revolution would be against the bureaucratic state itself.[38]

Two decades later, the Paris Commune reminded Marx of his prediction, which he proudly reported to Ludwig Kugelmann.[39] Arguably, his prediction was just a lucky guess, for the emergence of the Commune had little to do with his "scientific" theory of revolution, as Marx himself knew. Indeed, it was basically a product of both the political opportunity resulting from the military defeat of Napoleon III and of the imagination of the very utopians Marx had been castigating all along.

In any case, Marx now declared the Commune "the political form at last discovered under which to work out the economical emancipation of labor ..., a lever for uprooting the economical foundations upon which rests the existence of classes, and therefore of class rule."[40] As the events would soon prove, this was not a mere description of the now-crushed Commune; it was also a prescription for any future political rule of the proletariat.[41]

---

[37] "Marx to Joseph Weydemeyer, March 5, 1852," 62.

[38] Marx, *The Eighteenth Brumaire of Louis Bonaparte*, 185ff.

[39] "Marx to Ludwig Kugelmann, April 12, 1871," 131.

[40] Ibid., 334.

[41] In the postscript to a new edition of *The Civil War in France*, written eight years after Marx's death, Engels became the first known person to

To be fair, excepting the brief period alluded to above, Marx had consistently been anti-state since the early 1840s (see Chapter 3). "The working class cannot simply lay hold of ready-made state machinery and wield it for its own purposes," he says in the *Brumaire* (1852).[42] This was now "proved by the Commune."[43] What was thus "at last discovered" in 1871, according to Marx (but surely not in the minds of his radical French opponents), was the positive "political form" of working-class rule:

> The Paris Commune was, of course, to serve as a model to all the great industrial centers of France. The communal régime once established in Paris and the secondary centers, the old centralized Government would in the provinces, too, have to give way to the self-government of the producers. In a rough sketch of national organization which the Commune had no time to develop, it states clearly that the Commune was to be the political form of even the smallest country hamlet ... The rural communes of every district were to administer their common affairs by an assembly of delegates in the central town, and these district assemblies were again to send deputies to the National Delegation in Paris, each delegate to be at any time revocable and bound by the *mandat impératif* of his constituents. The few but important functions which still would remain for a central government were ... to be discharged by Communal, and therefore strictly responsible agents [made responsible by the institutions of revocation and imperative mandate]. The unity of the nation was not to be broken, but, on the contrary, to be organized by the Communal constitution.[44]

---

call the Commune a proletarian dictatorship: "Of late, the German [Social-Democratic] philistine has once more been filled with wholesome terror at the words: Dictatorship of the Proletariat. Well and good, gentlemen, do you want to know what this dictatorship looks like? Look at the Paris Commune. That was the Dictatorship of the Proletariat." Engels, "Introduction (to Karl Marx's *The Civil War in France*)," 191. I have little doubt that Marx would have agreed with this statement.

[42] Ibid., 328.

[43] Marx and Engels, "Preface to the 1872 German Edition of the *Manifesto of the Communist Party*," 175.

[44] Marx, *The Civil War in France*, 332.

Moreover, "the police was at once stripped of its political attributes, and turned into the responsible and at all times revocable agent of the Commune. So were the officials of all other branches of the Administration," Marx writes approvingly. He also speaks very favorably of the Commune's "suppression of the standing army, and the substitution for it of the armed people [i.e., national militia]." Lastly, "much "like the rest of public servants, magistrates and judges were to be elective, responsible, and revocable." And, "from the members of the Commune downwards, the public service had to be done at *workmen's wages*."[45]

Apparently, Marx here conceives the dictatorship of the proletariat as a state in some sense, even though it is to "become a reality by the destruction of the State power." This ambiguity anticipates Engels' later suggestion to Bebel that "All the palaver about the state ought to be dropped, especially after the Commune, which had ceased to be a state in the true sense of the term."[46] Marx makes a similar claim in his marginalia to Bakunin's *Statehood and Anarchy*.[47]

In short, I take it that the "true sense" of "the state" refers to that "centralized and organized governmental power usurping to be the master instead of the servant of society."[48] By contrast, the Commune was based on "really democratic institutions." In this sense, it was "the direct antithesis" to the bureaucratic state.[49] This is because the state as such "cannot serve as the political instrument of ... emancipation."[50] Only "really democratic institutions" can serve this end; the means and ends must coincide.

Marx continued to defend these views after 1871. For instance, we find strong traces of them in his conspectus (1874-1875) of Bakunin's *Statism and Anarchy*, in which the famed anarchist explicitly targets Marx, the "authoritarian." In his book, Bakunin rhetorically asks: "There are about 40 million Germans. Does this mean that all 40 million will be members of the government?" Marx responds: "CERTAINLY! For the system starts with the self-

[45] Ibid., 331.
[46] "Engels to August Bebel, March 18-28, 1875," 64.
[47] Marx, "Notes on Bakunin's Book *Statehood and Anarchy*," 519.
[48] Marx, "First Draft of *The Civil War in France*," 486-87.
[49] Marx, *The Civil War in France*, 334, 330.
[50] Marx, "Second Draft of *The Civil War in France*," 533.

government of the communities [or the communes]." The transitional nature of the *political* rule (or the dictatorship) of the proletariat is also reiterated: "When class rule has disappeared there [will] be no state in the present political sense." This means that the state, here strictly understood as the "class rule" of the proletariat, will remain during the initial phase of communism, until all *classes* wither away. The bureaucratic-machine state will be abolished immediately, however. Even after the disappearance of classes, and so of political rule, elections, based on "universal suffrage," will allow the denizens of the future society elect their representatives. Their "functions" will "become a routine matter which entails no domination." This may be called a "workers' state, if [Bakunin] wants to call it that." Marx also includes, in passim, "workers' co-operative" factories, etc., in his scheme of communism in his conspectus.[51]

The foregoing paragraphs help us understand the context in which Marx took the Lassalleans to task in his *Critique of the Gotha Program* (1875). In response to the declaration that the German Workers' party struggles for "the free state," Marx rhetorically asks: "Free state—what is this?" To Marx, the declaration smacks of Lassalle's Hegelian faith in the state as an independent, ethical entity. Instead of "treating existing society (and this holds good for any future one) as the [legitimate or ethical] *basis* of the existing state (or of the future state in the case of future society)," Marx protests, the program "treats the state rather as an independent entity that possesses its own intellectual, ethical, and libertarian bases." According to Marx, this *étatisme* requires "the narrow mentality of humble subjects." Therefore, "Freedom consists in converting the state from an organ superimposed upon society into one completely subordinate to it."[52]

Once more, Marx finds the bureaucratic state incompatible with *freedom*, proposing instead the demand for "*the revolutionary dictatorship of the proletariat*" to politically guide the transition from capitalism to communism.[53] He repeats these thoughts in an interview, published in *The Chicago Tribune* on January 5, 1879. In it, he once again takes a swipe at the Lassallean idea of "state aid

---

[51] Marx, "Notes on Bakunin's Book *Statehood and Anarchy*," 519-20.

[52] Marx, *Critique of the Gotha Program,* 94.

[53] Ibid., 95.

and credit for industrial [or co-operative] societies," even if this is to be undertaken "under democratic direction."[54]

To recapitulate, Marx identified the *future* "dictatorship of the proletariat" with expansive democracy, which he defined as the antithesis of the bureaucratic state. This dictatorship—or political rule, but not the "really democratic institutions," would disappear with the disappearance of classes. The chief task of this dictatorship, then, would be to bring about the economic and social self-emancipation of the working class. This includes the gradual abolition of all classes and, relatedly, allowing the spontaneous development of collective-cooperative ownership of the means of production. Having discussed it in the previous chapter, this feature of Marx's utopia will be taken for granted in what follows. The next section will discuss the relevant issue of how the collectively produced means of need-satisfaction (consumption) ought to be distributed in communism.

8.4 Distribution in Communism

Marx's most elaborate discussion of "fair distribution" in socialism is found in *The Critique of the Gotha Program*, and in response to the following demand in The Gotha Program: "'The emancipation of labor demands the raising of the means of labor to the common property of society and the collective regulation of the total labor with a fair distribution of the proceeds of labor.'"[55]

Everything in this sentence accords with Marx's longstanding views about socialism, except the "fair distribution" part. To this, he reacts viscerally, calling it "obsolete verbal rubbish," as well as a perversion of "the realistic outlook, which it cost so much effort [to Marx] to instill into the Party but which has now taken root in it, by means of ideological, legal and other trash so common among the Democrats and French Socialists."[56] The incoherence of his response to this issue is thus unsurprising.

Marx's incoherence is visible in the four rhetorical questions he poses, which may be fruitfully stated as propositions. "[T]he bourgeois assert that present-day distribution is 'fair'." What they assert is, "in fact, the only 'fair' distribution" in capitalism. This is

[54] Marx, "Account of Karl Marx's Interview with *The Chicago Tribune* Correspondent," 572. I added the [No!] for clarity.
[55] Marx, *Critique of the Gotha Program*, 83.
[56] Ibid., 87.

because "legal relations arise from economic ones." Lastly, "the socialist sectarians [also have] the most varied notions about 'fair' distribution."[57] Thus, he appears to be holding two contradictory views: The question of "fair" distribution (with or without the inverted commas) is both relative and absolute in some sense. In other words, when his fourth claim is considered together with the rest, he appears to be saying that there cannot be any agreement on the issue of fair distribution because it is subjectively determined differently, say, by "the bourgeoisie" and "the socialist sectarians." Without the fourth claim, he appears to be saying that "the bourgeois" view of fair distribution is the "only" valid-just one in capitalism," and this on moral-positivist grounds (see Chapter 4).

However, Marx's subsequent comments on this issue in the *Critique* suggests that he takes himself to be defending the latter, reductionist, implausible view: "Any distribution whatever of the means of consumption is only a consequence of the distribution of the conditions of production themselves." Thus, from the private ownership of the means of production in capitalism "the present-day distribution of the means of consumption results automatically. If the material conditions of production are the collective property of the workers themselves, then there likewise results [automatically] a distribution of the means of consumption different from the present one."[58]

This is not the place to revisit the problems associated with Marx's materialist automatism. Suffice it to note that his presentation of it here lends itself to the problematic notion that the program of a workers' party should not be concerned with the issue of the distribution of the means of consumption, for this will "result automatically" from the collective means of production. This materialist automatism also makes his demand for proletarian dictatorship in the *Critique* irrelevant.

In any case, Marx goes on to discuss the issue in some detail anyway. In addition to the issue of fairness, he finds problematic the "unscientific" Lassallean notion of "undiminished proceeds of labor," on which the Gotha Program rests its prescriptive claim that "the proceeds of labor belong undiminished with equal right to all members of society." In his anger, Marx also misconstrues this demand by assuming that it precludes deductions for public

---

[57] Ibid., 84.
[58] Ibid., 87-88.

expenditure. As he himself acknowledges in a different part of his *Critique*, the Program calls for free education and administration of criminal justice, etc.,[59] which obviously require deductions from "the proceeds of [total] labor." Differently put, the implication of the demand is that all deductions intended for public expenditure would return to "all members of society," one way or another.

In any case, Marx ridicules the authors of the Program for not having grasped the need for such deductions in socialism, and then reluctantly outlines his own scheme of distribution. He first gives a list of expenditures, which are to be deducted from "the total social product" in socialism. These include the cost of both replenishing the means of production and further expanding their capacity, a "reserve or insurance fund to provide against accidents, disturbances caused by natural factors, etc.," as well as the deductions needed to cover "the general costs of administration." Like the authors of the Program, he also anticipates additional deductions to pay for "that which is intended for the common satisfaction of needs, such as schools, health services, etc.," as well as "funds for those unable to work, etc." Marx tellingly expects (or rather desires) these expenditures to increase progressively "in proportion as the new society develops." These deductions benefit "the producer ... directly or indirectly in his capacity as a member of society," if not always "in his capacity as a private individual." After all these "deductions have been made," each individual producer of "the collective" is to receive "back from society ... exactly what he gives to it." The latter is to be determined by "the individual labor time of the individual producer."[60] Thus, after making much fuss about the language of "equal right" in the Program, Marx himself proposes almost the same principle of equal right.

This contribution-reward standard is also repeated in the second volume of *Capital*, though in a rather nonchalant manner: In the future socialist society, the "producers may, for all it matters, receive paper vouchers entitling them to withdraw from the social supplies of consumer goods a quantity corresponding to their labor time."[61] Likewise, he mentions the criterion of "labor time" as the principle of socialist distribution in the first volume of *Capital*.

---

[59] Ibid., 81, 96-97.
[60] Ibid., 84-85, 86.
[61] Marx, *Capital*, Vol. 2, 356.

Although he seems to "assume" this criterion analogously, "merely for the sake of a parallel with the production of commodities" (this phrase is replaced with the third ellipsis in the ensuing passage), it is very likely that he envisioned it as the distributive principle of socialism. This is likely because the discussion in which he presents it parallels closely the predictions (or rather the prescriptions) found in the *Critique*. The discussion in *Capital* runs as follows:

> Let us now picture ... a community of free individuals, carrying on their work with the means of production in common, in which the labor power of all the different individuals is consciously applied as the combined labor power of the community ... The total product of our [hypothetical] community is a social product. One portion [of this product] serves as fresh means of production and remains social. But another portion is consumed by the members as means of subsistence. A distribution of this portion amongst them is consequently necessary ... [T]he share of each individual producer in the means of subsistence is determined by his labor time.[62]

Marx does not say this principle of distribution is a transitional or "defective" principle in *Capital*. He does so in the *Critique*. In fact, he presents two versions of it, both of which he deems unsatisfactory. The first version would reward producers in accordance with "the labor they supply." "But," he protests, "one man is superior to another physically or mentally [skill-wise?] and so supplies more labor in the same time or can work for a longer time." If so, the standard "tacitly recognizes the unequal individual endowment and thus productive capacity of the workers as natural privileges. *It is, therefore, a right of inequality, in its content, like every right.*" The second version is based on some scheme of equal renumeration for equal hours worked, which would also produce inequality since each producer has different or unequal social and natural needs. "To avoid all these defects, right would have to be unequal rather than equal."[63]

This insightful argument is devastating to Marx's own "realistic

[62] Marx, *Capital*, Vol. 1, 89.
[63] Marx, *Critique of the Gotha Program*, 86-87. For an illuminating discussion, see Moore, *Marx on the Choice between Socialism and Communism*, 45ff

outlook" because it is ethically grounded. In other words, he calls these equalitarian standards of distribution "defective" on the ground that they take "individuals ... from a *certain* side only," regarding them "*only as workers*" or producers, ignoring "everything else" about them.[64] Therefore, the standard of "equal right" fails to recognize each person as a human being, with different needs and abilities.

Here, a hierarchy of principles emerges. The *communistic* principle(s) of "equal right" is still an "advance" over the "fair" principle of exchange-distribution prevalent in bourgeois society. This is because it "recognizes no class distinctions." Relatedly, its implementation would mean that "nothing can pass to the ownership of individuals except individual means of consumption."[65] This claim recalls the following statement from the *Manifesto*: "Communism deprives no man of the power to appropriate the products of society; all that it does is to deprive him of the power to subjugate the labor of others by means of such appropriations."[66] This helps clarify why Marx thinks the socialistic principle is an "advance" upon the "bourgeois" principle of distribution in the *Critique*; it is an ethically-grounded clarification, which values freedom.

Still, as noted above, both equalitarian-communistic standard(s) produces defects, largely because it reduces individuals to one-sided abstractions, ignoring their varied needs and abilities as human beings. "These defects," Marx goes on to argue famously, "are inevitable in the first [or initial] phase of communist society as it is when it has just emerged after prolonged birth-pangs from capitalist society. Right can never be higher than the economic structure of society and its cultural development which this [structure] determines."[67]

As we see, he is unwilling to part with his reductionist "realistic outlook," which implies that he here simply predicts the arrival of the "higher" communistic principle or right, rather than desiring or prescribing it. This further implies that he has no preference for any principle of distribution, and—pushing this implication to its logical

---

[64] Ibid., 87.
[65] Ibid., 86.
[66] Marx and Engels, *Manifesto of the Communist Party*, 500.
[67] Ibid., 87.

Communism: The Realm of Freedom

conclusion—for any form of society whatsoever. It also makes nonsense of his ranking of principles as "defective" etc.

In the interest of coherence, then, I read the following passage as an ethically grounded prescription:

> In a higher phase of communist society, after the enslaving subordination of the individual to the division of labor, and thereby also the antithesis between mental and physical labor, has vanished; after labor has become not only a means of life but life's prime want [or need]; after the productive forces have also increased with the all-round development of the individual, and all the springs of common wealth flow more abundantly—only then can the narrow horizon of bourgeois right be crossed in its entirety and society inscribe on its banner: From each according to his abilities, to each according to his needs![68]

This passage certainly offers an image of the Marxian good society. "If it is utopian to have an image of the good society, then indeed Marx and Engels may rightly be included among the ranks of utopian socialists."[69] Interestingly, Marx borrowed the abilities-needs principle from the socialist utopians.[70]

Even less known is the fact that Marx and Engels had used various formulations of it previously. For example, different formulations of it are discussed in some detail in *The German Ideology*.[71] Indeed, the logic behind the "higher" needs-principle is

---

[68] Ibid.

[69] Levitas, *The Concept of Utopia*, 45. Levitas does not mention this complication, and so assumes readily that "the difference between Marxism and utopian socialism does not rest on the existence or otherwise of an image of the socialist society to be attained, nor even on the content of that image. It rests upon disagreements about the process of transition" (ibid.).

[70] For an impressive survey of the origins of the slogan, see Bovens and Lutz, "'From Each according to Ability; To Each according to Needs': Origin, Meaning, and Development of Socialist Slogans," 237-57. Also see Manuel and Manuel, *Utopian Thought in the Western World*. 710ff.

[71] Marx and Engels, *The German Ideology*, 505ff. Among the two, the full version of the double-principle was first quoted by Engels in 1851, giving Louis Blanc as its source. Engels, "Critical Review of Proudhon's Book, *Idée générale de la révolution au XIXe siècle*," 555.

146

elaborated upon in a seldom-noticed passage in this text. It is a humanist-ethical logic, as far as I am concerned:

> But one of the most vital principles of communism, a principle which distinguishes it from all reactionary socialism, is its empirical view, based on a knowledge of man's nature, that differences of *brain* and of intellectual ability do not imply any differences whatsoever in the nature of the *stomach* and of physical *needs*; therefore the false tenet, based upon existing circumstances, "to each according to his abilities", must be changed, insofar as it relates to enjoyment in its narrower sense, into the tenet, "*to each according to his need*"; in other words, a *different form* of [ability, of] activity, of labor, does not justify *inequality*, confers no *privileges* in respect of possession and enjoyment.[72]

For the most part, this passage speaks for itself. However, the implied justification of the preferred communistic principle, "*to each according to his need,*" needs to be stressed. Its justification is "based on a knowledge of man's nature." This is to say, each is entitled to satisfy his or her needs by virtue of being human. In another section of *The German Ideology*, this entitlement is called the "the first premise of all human existence," which is that "men must be in a position to live," and this "involves before everything else eating and drinking, housing, clothing and various other things."[73]

Furthermore, especially in the *Critique*, the principle is understood in *transitional* terms, contingent upon further technological and cultural development. This is a reasonable assumption, except when it is confused with the materialist automatism. As such, it is not as absurdly optimistic as it is supposed by some of Marx's critics. "From each according to his abilities" is likewise a transitional principle. As the famous passage from the *Critique* clearly suggests, it also hinges on another cardinal principle, namely, "the all-round development of the individual," to issue from free, all-round activity of the same—according to the abilities of each.

---

[72] Marx and Engels, *The German Ideology*, 537.
[73] Ibid., 41-42.

8.5 Freedom and Self-Realization

Let us begin this section with a clarification, which has already been made several times throughout this study. Marx does not ultimately rest his case for the abolition of the alienated "free labor" on the tendency of capitalism to lower the wages of workers or on the socialistic desideratum to increase them. As he puts it in the *Manuscripts of 1844*, "An enforced *increase of wages* ... would ... be nothing but *better payment for the slave* and would not win for the worker or for labor their human status and dignity."[74]

Likewise, against those who argue that they will have higher wages if capital grows rapidly, Marx retorts in "Wage Labor and Capital" that this, if realized, would also mean the growth of "the power that is hostile" to, and "rules over," workers. Among other things, this means to him that higher wages would be tantamount to the "golden chains by which the bourgeoisie drags [workers] in its train."[75]

Similarly, and apropos the issue of equalitarian principles of distribution, Marx argues in "Value, Price, and Profit" that "To clamor for equal or even equitable retribution on the basis of the wages system is the same as to clamor for freedom on the basis of the slavery system." The more fundamental task is to abolish the present-day "system of production," which is based upon the modern system of slavery.[76] Thus, "Instead of the conservative motto, '*A fair day's wage for a fair day's work!*'" workers "ought to inscribe on their banner the revolutionary watchword, '*Abolition of the wages system!*'"[77]

The issue of adequate or fair wages reappears in the *Critique*, specifically in opposition to the Lassallean "iron law of wages." According to this "iron and cruel law" (Lassalle), wages necessarily remain at the mere subsistence level in capitalism. Thus, capitalism must be abolished for this reason. "It is as if," Marx retorts wryly, "among slaves who have at last got behind the secret of slavery and broken out in rebellion, a slave still in thrall to obsolete notions were to inscribe on the program of the rebellion: Slavery must be abolished because the feeding of slaves in the system of slavery

---

[74] Karl Marx, *Economic and Philosophic Manuscripts of 1844*, 280.
[75] Marx, "Wage Labor and Capital," 221
[76] Marx, "Value, Price, and Profit," 129.
[77] Ibid., 148-49.

cannot exceed a certain low maximum!"[78] Otherwise put, I presume, a revolutionary workers' program should instead read: *Capitalism must be abolished because it is a system of slavery*.

At least two related questions need to be asked before we proceed any further: What kind of freedom? Why freedom? In the *Critique*, as we have seen in the previous section, Marx describes-prescribes the "higher" phase of communism as a community in which the "enslaving" division of labor in capitalism, including "the antithesis between mental and physical labor," would be transcended, giving way to "all-round" free activity. Crucially, he calls the latter "life's prime want," by which he means a vital human need (*Lebensbedürfnis*).

These comments answer our questions, at least partially. With the findings of Chapter 1 also in mind, I once more reiterate that Marx necessarily derives the principle of freedom from his conception of human nature. Thus, freedom is necessary because its presence satisfies a vital human need. This issue will reemerge shortly. Let us now consider further what he meant, and did not mean, by all-around activity.

In a "communist society," we read in *The German Ideology*,

> nobody has one exclusive sphere of activity but each can become accomplished in any branch he wishes, society regulates the general production and thus makes it possible for me to do one thing today and another tomorrow, to hunt in the morning, fish in the afternoon, rear cattle in the evening, criticize after dinner, just as I have a mind, without ever becoming hunter, fisherman, herdsman or critic.[79]

This apparent portrayal of communism by Engels as a preindustrial utopia has puzzled many scholars. Also, it is supposed that its underlying principle was deemed silly by Marx.[80] This view

---

[78] Marx, *Critique of the Gotha Program*, 92.

[79] Marx and Engels, *The German Ideology*, 46–48.

[80] *Pace* Carver, "Communism for Critical Critics? 'The German Ideology' and the Problem of Technology." Rockmore defends a similar position, readily doubting Marx's acceptance of the passage on the ground that it implies dispensing with "division of labor," which is too "utopian, hence inconsistent with Marx's strong social realism." Rockmore, *Marx's Dream: From Capitalism to Communism*, 64. I fail to see how the passage implies doing away with division of labor *tout court*.

cannot explain the fact that its underlying principle, which is what really matters, is defended by Marx, *solo*, elsewhere and repeatedly. This idea is encapsulated in the words "just as I have a mind."

In other words, neither the number of activities nor what these activities specifically are is the crucial aspect of the communistic desideratum of all-round activity. Rather, it rests on the principle that these activities must be self-posited. Another key prerequisite for this criterion is the absence of structurally imposed professions in communism. One hunts, etc., "without ever becoming hunter," etc. "In a communist society, there are no painters but only people who engage in painting among other activities."[81]

In the first volume of *Capital*, Marx similarly explains how modern industry, in its capitalist form, "necessitates variation of labor, fluency of function, universal mobility of the laborer, on the other hand ..., [and] reproduces the old division of labor with its ossified particularizations," on the other hand. This problem cannot be solved in capitalism, though the material and social conditions it has created points to the negation of this negation.[82] In other words, capitalism also makes possible the individual "to whom the different social functions he performs, are but so many modes of giving free scope to his own natural and acquired powers.[83]

Unlike what some scholars claim, Marx's idea of all-around activity does not exclude division of labor altogether. Defined in one sense as a freely *cooperative* society, the concept of communism necessarily implies some form of division of labor.[84] Otherwise, one would have to argue, as per impossible, that Marx conceived communism as a society of Robinson Crusoes, each performing, in isolation, "useful work of various sorts, such as making tools and furniture, taming goats, fishing and hunting."[85] After describing Crusoe's activities in this way, Marx tellingly transports him to a *hypothetical* "community of free individuals, carrying on their work with the means of production in common, in which the labor power

---

[81] Marx and Engels, *The German Ideology*, 292.

[82] Marx, *Capital*, Vol. 1, 489-90.

[83] Ibid., 490-91.

[84] For sound rebuttals of the untrue claim, and informed explanations of the senses in which division of labor remains in Marx's Communism, see Wallimann, *Estrangement*, Ch. 7; Ware, "Marx, the Division of Labor, and Human Nature," esp. 57ff.

[85] Marx, *Capital*, Vol. 1, 87.

of all the different individuals is consciously applied as the combined labor power of the community. All the characteristics of Robinson's labor are here repeated [including division of labor], but with this difference, that they are social, instead of individual."[86] By "social," he here means production for the sake of each and all.

In any case, the goal of maximizing all-around activity is consistent with Marx's aim to maximize freedom. It also informs his desideratum of human flourishing, based upon the freedom of "every person ... to achieve all-round development of all *his* abilities."[87] Engels declares this sort of freedom as the *principle* of "the Communists" (read Marx and Engels) in the "Draft of a Communist Confession of Faith," written shortly after he and Marx had jointly penned down *The German Ideology*. These "Communists" declare, as one of their chief aims, the organization of "society in such a way that every member of it can develop and use all his capabilities and powers in complete freedom and without thereby infringing the basic conditions of this society."[88] To wit, this is the harm principle of these two "Communists."

This thought dovetails another passage from *The German Ideology*: "Only within the [true or real] community has each individual the means of cultivating his gifts in all directions; hence personal freedom becomes possible only within the community," not the "illusory community" in which one class not only dominates and exploits the others but also monopolizes the means of self-realization. In short, "In the real community the individuals obtain their freedom in and through their association."[89] In the *Manifesto*, we read: "In place of the old bourgeois society ..., we shall have an association, in which the free development of each is the precondition for the development of all."[90] These comments point to the *opposite* of the notion of "self-realization of the individual for the sake of community,"[91] or the conception of a society in which individuality would disappear altogether.[92]

---

[86] Ibid., 89.

[87] Marx and Engels, *The German Ideology*, 292.

[88] Engels, "Draft of a Communist Confession of Faith," 96. Also see Engels, "Principles of Communism," 353.

[89] Marx and Engels, *The German Ideology*, 78.

[90] Ibid., 506.

[91] *Pace* Elster, *Making Sense of Marx*, 446.

[92] For a lengthy list of authors who defend this view, and their judicious refutation, see Nordahl, "Marx and Utopia."

Marx also argues crucially in the *Grundrisse* that "the absolute unfolding of man's creative abilities [or potentialities]" is not to be "measured by any *previously given [or predetermined] yardstick*." Rather, "the development of all human powers as such" is to be posited as "the end-in-itself." Here, "the end" has a double reference. On the one hand, it refers to making the self-actualization of human nature, of human potentialities, in a word, "man" himself, the purpose (end) of production and wealth. At the same time, it refers to a goal, which is also not "a *predetermined yardstick*." In other words, in communism, "man" "does not reproduce himself in any specific character but produces his totality ...; does not seek to remain something he has already become but is in the absolute movement of becoming."[93]

If so, unlike what some scholars would have us believe, Marx leaves the issue of human development open-ended, wisely presupposing no specific minimum or maximum limit. With this passage in mind, Benhabib judiciously captures the essence of Marx's principle: It "expresses in a nutshell the normative ideal underlying Marx's critique of capitalism," as well as his "vision" of "an active" self-transforming humanity.[94]

The urge and potential to develop is intrinsic to human nature, Marx must have assumed. This would explain his objection to Adam Smith's reduction of freedom and happiness to "rest." "It does not seem remotely to occur to him," retorts Marx, "that the individual 'in his ordinary state of health, strength, spirits, skill, dexterity' also needs a normal portion of labor and the transcendence of 'rest'." Equally, "A. Smith has no inkling that the overcoming of ... obstacles is in itself a manifestation of freedom," especially when such acts or works are self-posited, and so become processes of "self-realization, objectification of the subject, and thus real freedom." Such self-posited acts, Marx adds, "become *travail attractif*," *even if* they demand "the most intensive effort."[95]

According Marx, free activity can be further enhanced with the reduction of the time required for necessary labor or, which is the same thing, the increase of free, disposable time. He calculates that the expansion of free time is already possible in capitalism, in which

---

[93] Marx, *Outlines of the Critique of Political Economy, MECW* 28: 411-12.
[94] Benhabib, *Critique, Norm, and Utopia*, 112-13.
[95] Marx, *Outlines of the Critique of Political Economy, MECW* 28: 529-30.

there occurs, on the one hand, the conversion of labor from direct production to overseeing and regulation (due to mechanization, etc.) and the *"theft of alien labor time,"* on which the present wealth turns. In any case, such conditions as these point to the possibility of "the reduction of the necessary labor of society," which would then make possible "the artistic, scientific, etc., development of individuals," that is, "free development of individualities."[96] A few pages later, Marx again reiterates, "the increase of free time" makes possible the "development of the individual."[97] These comments presuppose the crucial link between free, all-around activity and all-around development of the individual.

Marx discusses the issue of free time also in his *Economic Manuscript of 1861-63.* "FREE TIME, *DISPOSABLE TIME,*" he stresses in capitalized letters, "is wealth itself, partly for the enjoyment of the product, partly for FREE ACTIVITY which—unlike LABOR—is not determined by a compelling extraneous purpose which must be fulfilled, and the fulfilment of which is regarded as a natural necessity or a social duty, according to one's inclination." Here, but not always, Marx distinguishes (genuine) free activity from *labor*, which refers to socially necessary activity of production. However, in communism, even necessary labor is free in comparison to its historical counterparts, in the sense that it "is no longer performed for someone else," and so does not entail "the social contradictions between MASTER AND MEN." In communism, this form of labor thus "acquires a quite different, a free character" since "it becomes truly social [i.e., without any masters] labor."[98] So, socially necessary productive activity in communism is also free in this sense.

Marx makes a similar distinction between the two types of *free* activity in the third volume of *Capital.* He reasons that "labor which is determined by necessity and mundane considerations" cannot be completely eradicated in any mode of production, including developed communism.[99] Yet, and once again, he does not regard such labor unfree; nor does he assume that it is either alienating or

---

[96] Marx, *Economic Manuscript of 1861-63*, *MECW* 32, 91.

[97] Ibid., 97. "Truly" is substituted for "real."

[98] Ibid., 391.

[99] Marx, *Capital*, Vol. 3, 807. In the *Manuscripts of* 1844, he seems to have a more optimistic view in this regard.

fails to count as self-realization and development,[100] though what he means is not very precise.

"Freedom in this field," Marx clarifies once more, "can only consist in socialized man, the associated producers, rationally [and collectively] regulating their interchange with Nature." Yet, "it nonetheless still remains a realm of necessity." "In fact," he maintains, "the realm of [true] freedom actually begins only where labor which is determined by necessity and mundane considerations ceases; thus in the very nature of things it lies beyond the sphere of [necessity]." In this sphere is found "that development of human energy, which is an end in itself." This is "the true realm of freedom," and "the shortening of the working day is its basic prerequisite."[101] As we see, Marx once again thinks of the communistic goals in transitional terms.

Moreover, Marx here defines truly free activity as self-posited activity that the individual regards as an "end in itself," as opposed to the kind of free activity that is instrumental to the satisfaction of material needs or other external purposes. This distinction is also made by the young Marx: The animal "produces only under the dominion of immediate physical need, whilst man produces even when he is free from physical need and only truly produces in freedom therefrom."[102]

Clearly, Marx's distinction, and the exaltation of the former above the latter, calls to mind Aristotle's distinction between *praxis* and *poesis*, though pursuing this connection here would require an extensive treatment. Suffice it to note that, like Aristotle, Marx regards free activity as a human good. He accordingly stresses in the third volume of *Capital* that freedom of individuals should be achieved "under conditions most favorable to, and worthy of, their human nature."[103] Indeed, this is the philosophical definition of communism.

---

[100] The contrary view is defended in Cohen, "Marx's Dialectic of Labor," and in Marcuse, "The Realm of Freedom and the Realm of Necessity." For a convincing rebuttal of the contrary view, see Klagge, "Marx's Realms of 'Freedom' and 'Necessity'." Also see Kandiyali, "Freedom and Necessity in Marx's Account of Communism."

[101] Marx, *Capital*, Vol. 3, 807.

[102] Marx, *Economic and Philosophic Manuscripts of 1844*, 276.

[103] Marx, *Capital*, Vol. 3, 807.

***

Once we bracket out the claims and predictions of the "scientific" Marx, what remains is a philosophy of revolution, which is ultimately a humanist philosophy of self-emancipation. As such, it prescribes the abolition of capitalism on ethical grounds. It conceives the revolutionary transition from capitalism (the sphere of alienation) to communism (the sphere of freedom) as a process of dealienation or self-emancipation. Capitalism, therefore, "disappears with ... [the disappearance of] alienation."[104]

Relatedly, communism is conceived, prescribed, and desired as the realm of freedom. As such, and to repeat Marx's words with a slight modification, communism is the general economic, social, and political condition "*most favorable to, and worthy of* ..., *human nature* [emphasis added]."[105] If so, "*Communism* is the *positive* transcendence of ... *human self-estrangement,* and therefore ... [is] the real *appropriation* of the *human* essence by and for man."[106] This, once again, is the crux of Marx's humanist revolutionary philosophy of freedom.

---

[104] Marx, *Economic Manuscript of 1861-63*, *MECW* 32: 446.

[105] Marx, *Capital*, Vol. 3, 807.

[106] Marx, *Economic and Philosophic Manuscripts of 1844*, 296.

References

Althusser, Louis. *Lenin and Philosophy and Other Essays*. New York: Monthly Review Press, 1971.

Aristotle. *Nicomachean Ethics*. In *The Complete Works of Aristotle*, Vol. 2, edited by Jonathan Barnes. Princeton: Princeton University Press, 1984.

Avineri, Shlomo. *The Social and Political Thought of Karl Marx*. Cambridge: Cambridge University Press, 1968.

Bakunin, Michael. *Bakunin on Anarchy: Selected Works by the Activist-Founder of World Anarchism*. Edited and translated by Sam Dolgoff. New York: Vintage Books, 1971

———. *The Political Philosophy of Bakunin: Scientific Anarchism*. Edited by G. P Maximof. New York: The Free Press, 1953.

Benhabib, Seyla. *Critique, Norm, and Utopia: A Study of the Foundations of Critical Theory* New York: Columbia University Press, 1986.

Bernstein, Eduard. *Selected Writings, 1900–1921*. Edited and translated by Manfred Steger. Atlantic Highlands: Humanities Press, 1996.

Berthier, René. *Social-Democracy and Anarchism: In the International Workers Association, 1864-1877*. Translated by A. W. Zurbrügg. London: Merlin Press, 2015.

Bidet, Jacques. *Exploring Marx's Capital: Philosophical, Economic, and Political Dimensions*. Chicago: Haymarket Books, 2009.

Blackburn, Robin. *Marx and Lincoln: An Unfinished Revolution*. London: Verso, 2011.

Blaisdell, Lowell L. "Félix Pyat, the 'Evil Genius' of the Commune of Paris." *Proceedings of the American Philosophical Society* 132, no. 4 (1988): 330-70.

Bovens, Luc and Adrien Lutz. "'From Each according to Ability; To Each according to Needs': Origin, Meaning, and Development of Socialist Slogans." *History of Political Economy* 51, no. 2 (2019): 237-57.

Brenkert, George G. *Marx's Ethics of Freedom*. London: Routledge & Kegan Paul, 1983.

Carver, Terrell. "Communism for Critical Critics? 'The German Ideology' and the Problem of Technology." *History of Political Thought* 9, no. 1 (1988): 129-136.

References

Chattopadhyay, Paresh. *Socialism and Commodity Production: Essay in Marx Revival*. Leiden: Brill, 2018.

Chitty, Andrew. "The Early Marx on Needs." *Radical Philosophy* 64, no. 2 (1993): 23-31.

Cohen, G. A. "Historical Inevitability and Human Agency in Marxism." *Proceedings of the Royal Society of London* 407, no. 1832 (1986), 65-87.

———. *Karl Marx's Theory of History: A Defence*. Expanded edition. Princeton: Princeton University Press, 2000 (1978).

———. "Marx's Dialectic of Labor." In *Philosophy & Public Affairs* 3, no.3 (1974): 235-61.

———. "Review of Wood's *Karl Marx*." *Mind* 92, no. 367 (1983): 440-45.

Das, Raju J. "Marxist Theories of the State." In *Alternative Theories of the State*, edited by Steven Pressman, 64-90. Basingstoke: Palgrave Macmillan, 2006.

Draper, Hal. *Karl Marx's Theory of Revolution, Volume III: The "Dictatorship of the Proletariat."* New York: Monthly Review Press, 1986.

———. *Karl Marx's Theory of Revolution: State and Bureaucracy*. New York: Monthly Review Press, 1977.

Dunayevskaya, Raya. "Marx's Humanism Today." In *Socialist Humanism: An International Symposium*, edited by Erich Fromm. Garden City: Doubleday, 1965.

———. *Marxism and Freedom*. London: Pluto Press, 1971.

Eckhardt, Wolfgang. *The First Socialist Schism: Bakunin vs. Marx in the International Working Men's Association*. Translated by Robert M. Homsi, Jesse Cohn, Cian Lawless, Nestor McNab, and Bas Moreel. Oakland: PM Press, 2016.

Edara, Dileep. *Biography of a Blunder: Base and Superstructure in Marx and Later*. Newcastle upon Tyne: Cambridge Scholar Publishing, 2016.

Edwards, Stewart. *The Paris Commune, 1871*. New York: Quadrangle Books, 1971.

Elster, Jon. *An Introduction to Karl Marx*. Cambridge: Cambridge University Press, 1986.

———. *Making Sense of Marx*. Cambridge: Cambridge University Press, 1985.

Engels, Frederick. *Anti-Dühring: Herr Eugen Dühring's Revolution in Science*. In *Marx and Engels Collected Works*, Vol. 25. Moscow: Progress Publishers, 1987.

References

——. "Critical Review of Proudhon's Book, *Idée générale de la révolution au XIXe siècle*" In *Marx and Engels Collected Works*. Vol. 11. Moscow: Progress Publishers, 1979.

——. "Draft of a Communist Confession of Faith." In *Marx and Engels Collected Works*, Vol. 6. Moscow: Progress Publishers, 1976.

——. "Engels to August Bebel, March 18-28, 1875." In *Marx and Engels Collected Works*, Vol. 24, Moscow: Progress Publishers, 1989.

——. "Engels to Eduard Bernstein, October 25, 1881." In *Marx and Engels Collected Works*, Vol. 46. Moscow: Progress Publishers, 1992.

——. "Engels to Eduard Bernstein, November 2-3, 1882." In *Marx and Engels Collected Works*. Vol. 46. Moscow: Progress Publishers, 1992.

——. "Engels to Joseph Bloch, September 21-22, 1890." In *Marx and Engels Collected Works*, Vol. 49. Moscow: Progress Publishers, 2001.

——. "Engels to Karl Marx, September 30, 1868." In *Marx and Engels Collected Works*, Vol. 21. Moscow: Progress Publishers, 1985.

——. "Engels to Karl Marx, October 6, 1868." In *Marx and Engels Collected Works*, Vol. 21. Moscow: Progress Publishers, 1985.

——. "Engels to Karl Marx, September 12, 1870." In *Marx and Engels Collected Works*, Vol. 44. Moscow: Progress Publishers, 1989.

——. "Introduction (to Marx's *The Civil War in France*)." In *Marx and Engels Collected Works*, Vol. 27. Moscow: Progress Publishers, 1990.

——. "Introduction (to Marx's *The Class Struggles in France, 1848 to 1850*)." In *Marx and Engels Collected Works*, Vol. 27. Moscow: Progress Publishers, 1990.

——. "On The History of the Communist League." In *Marx and Engels Collected Works*, Vol. 26. Moscow: Progress Publishers, 1990.

——. *Origin of the Family, Private Property, and State.* In *Marx and Engels Collected Works*, Vol. 26. Moscow: Progress Publishers, 1990.

——. "Preface to the 1888 English Edition of *Manifesto of The Communist Party*." In *Marx and Engels Collected Works*, Vol. 26. Moscow: Progress Publishers, 1990.

——. "Principles of Communism." In *Marx and Engels Collected Works*, Vol. 6. Moscow: Progress Publishers, 1976.

——. "The Communists and Karl Heinzen." In *Marx and Engels Collected Works* Vol. 6. Moscow: Progress Publishers, 1976.

References

Feuerbach, Ludwig. "Preliminary Theses on the Reform of Philosophy." In *German Socialist Philosophy*, edited by Wolfgang Schirmacher. New York: Continuum, 1997.

Fromm, Erich. *Marx's Concept of Man*. New York: Frederick Ungar Publishing Co., 1961.

Geoghegan, Vincent. *Utopianism and Marxism*. Oxford: Peter Lang, 2008 (1987).

Geras, Norman. *Marx and Human Nature: Refutation of a Legend* (London: Verso, 1983), 90.

———. "Marxism and Proletarian Self-Emancipation." *Radical Philosophy* 6 (1973): 20-22.

Gogol, Eugene. *Toward a Dialectic of Philosophy and Organization*. Chicago: Haymarket Books, 2013.

Groff, Ruth. "On the Ethical Contours of Thin Aristotelian Marxism." In *Constructing Marxist Ethics: Critique, Normativity, Praxis*, 313-35, edited by Michael J. Thompson. Leiden: Brill, 2015.

Harvey, David. *A Companion to Marx's Capital*. London: Verso: 2013.

Hegel, G. W. F. *Elements of the Philosophy of Right*. Edited by Allen W. Wood and translated by H. B. Nisbet. Cambridge: Cambridge University Press, 1991.

Heller, Agnes. *The Theory of Need in Marx*. London: Allison & Busby, 1976.

Hobbes, Thomas. *Leviathan*. Edited by J. C. A. Gaskin. Oxford: Oxford University Press, 1996.

Horie, Tadao. *Marx's Capital and One Free World: A Fundamental Reappraisal of His Political Economy*. New York: Palgrave Macmillan, 1991.

Hudis, Peter. *Marx's Concept of the Alterative to Communism*. Chicago: Haymarket Books, 2012.

Hunt, Richard N. *Marx and Engels: Marxism and Totalitarian Democracy, 1818-1850*. Pittsburg: University of Pittsburgh Press 1974.

Husami, Ziyad I. "Marx on Distributive Justice." *Philosophy & Public Affairs* 8, no. 1 (1978): 27-64.

Kain, Philip J. *Marx and Ethics*. Oxford: Oxford University Press, 1988.

Kamenka, Eugene. *The Ethical Foundations of Marxism*, 2nd ed. rev. London, Routledge & Kegan Paul, 1972.

Kandiyali, Jan. "Freedom and Necessity in Marx's Account of Communism." In *British Journal for the History of Philosophy* 22, no. 1 (2014): 104–23.

References

Karatani, Kojin. *Transcritique: On Kant and Marx*. Translated by Sabu Kohso. Cambridge: The MIT Press, 2005).

Kautsky, Karl. *Ethics and the Materialist Conception of History*. Chicago: Charles H. Kerr, 1907.

Klagge, James C. "Marx's Realms of 'Freedom' and 'Necessity'." In *Canadian Journal of Philosophy* 16, no. 4 (1986): 769-77.

Kolakowski, Leszek. *Main Currents of Marxism: The Founders*, Volume 1. Oxford: Oxford University Press, 1978.

Lawrence, Ken. *Marx on American Slavery*. Tugaloo: Sojourner Truth Organization, 1976.

Lee, Donald C. "The Concept of 'Necessity': Marx and Marcuse." *The Southwestern Journal of Philosophy* 6, no. 1 (1975), 47-53.

Lefort, Claude. *Democracy and Political Theory*. Minneapolis: University of Minnesota Press, 1988.

Levitas, Ruth. *The Concept of Utopia*. Syracuse: Syracuse University Press, 1990.

Löwy, Michael. *The Theory of Revolution in the Young Marx*. Chicago: Haymarket Books, 2005.

Lukes, Steven. *Marxism and Morality*. New York: Oxford University Press, 1985.

———. "Marxism and Utopianism." In *Utopias*, edited by Peter Alexander and Roger Gill. London: Gerald Duckworth and Co, Ltd., 1984.

Mandel, Ernest. *Power and Money: A Marxist Theory of Bureaucracy*. London: Verso, 1992.

———. *The Formation of the Economic Thought of Karl Marx, 1843 to Capital*. Translated by Brian Pearce. New York: Monthly Review Press, 1971.

Manuel, Frank E. and Fritzie P. Manuel. *Utopian Thought in the Western World*. Cambridge: Harvard University Press, 1979.

Marcuse, Herbert. The Realm of Freedom and the Realm of Necessity: A Reconsideration." In *Praxis* 5, no. 1 (1969): 20-25.

Marx, Karl. "Account of Karl Marx's Interview with *The Chicago Tribune* Correspondent." In *Marx and Engels Collected Works*, Vol. 24. Moscow: Progress Publishers, 1989.

———. "Address of the International Workingmen's Association to Abraham Lincoln, President of the United States of America. Presented to U.S. Ambassador Charles Francis Adams on January 28, 1865." In *Marx and Engels Collected Works*, Vol. 20. Moscow: Progress Publishers, 1985.

References

———. *A Contribution to the Critique of Political Economy*. In *Marx and Engels Collected Works*, Vol. 29. Moscow: Progress Publishers, 1987.

———. *Capital: A Critical Analysis of Capitalist Production, London 1887*. Berlin: Dietz Verlag, 1990.

———. *Capital*, Volume 1. In *Marx and Engels Collected Works*, Vol. 35. Moscow: Progress Publishers, 1996.

———. *Capital*, Volume 2. In *Marx and Engels Collected Works*, Vol. 36. Moscow: Progress Publishers, 1997.

———. *Capital*, Volume 3. In *Marx and Engels Collected Works*, Vol. 37. Moscow: Progress Publishers, 1998.

———. "Contribution to the Critique of Hegel's Philosophy of Law." In *Marx and Engels Collected Works*, Vol. 3. Moscow: Progress Publishers, 1975.

———. "Contribution to the Critique of Hegel's Philosophy of Law: Introduction." In *Marx and Engels Collected Works*, Vol. 3. Moscow: Progress Publishers, 1975.

———. "Critical Marginal Notes on the Article 'The King of Prussia and Social Reform' by a Prussian." In *Marx and Engels Collected Works*, Vol. 3. Moscow: Progress Publishers, 1975.

———. *Critique of the Gotha Program*. In *Marx and Engels Collected Works*, Vol. 24. Moscow: Progress Publishers, 1989.

———. "Debates on Freedom of the Press and Publication of the Proceedings of the Assembly of the Estates." In *Marx and Engels Collected Works*, Vol. 1. Moscow: Progress Publishers, 1975.

———. "Draft of an Article on Friedrich List's Book *Das nationale System der politischen Oekonomie*." In *Marx and Engels Collected Works*, Vol. 4. Moscow: Progress Publishers, 1975.

———. "Draft Resolution of the General Council on the 'French Federal Section in London'." In *Marx and Engels Collected Works*, Vol. 21. Moscow: Progress Publishers, 1985.

———. *Economic and Philosophic Manuscripts of 1844*. In *Marx and Engels Collected Works*, Vol. 3. Moscow: Progress Publishers, 1975.

———. *Economic Manuscript of 1861-63*. In *Marx and Engels Collected Works*, Vol. 30. Moscow: Progress Publishers, 1988.

———. *Economic Manuscript of 1861-63*. In *Marx and Engels Collected Works*, Vol. 31. Moscow: Progress Publishers, 1989.

———. *Economic Manuscript of 1861-63*. In *Marx and Engels Collected Works*, Vol. 32. Moscow: Progress Publishers, 1989.

References

——. *Economic Manuscript of 1861-63*. In *Marx and Engels Collected Works*, Vol. 33. Moscow: Progress Publishers, 1991.

——. *Economic Manuscript of 1861-63*. In *Marx and Engels Collected Works*, Vol. 34. Moscow: Progress Publishers, 1994.

——. "First Draft of *The Civil War in France*." In *Marx and Engels Collected Works*, Vol. 22. Moscow: Progress Publishers, 1986.

——. "Inaugural Address of the Working Men's International Association." In *Marx and Engels Collected Works*, Vol. 20. Moscow: Progress Publishers, 1985.

——. "Instructions for the Delegates of the Provisional General Council. The Different Questions." In *Marx and Engels Collected Works*, Vol. 20. Moscow: Progress Publishers, 1985.

——. "Marginal Notes on Adolph Wagner's *Lehrbuch der politischen Oekonomie*." In *Marx and Engels Collected Works*, Vol. 24. Moscow: Progress Publishers, 1989.

——. "Marx to Arnold Ruge, September 1843." In *Marx and Engels Collected Works*, Vol. 3. Moscow: Progress Publishers, 1975.

——. "Marx to Carlo Cafiero, July 29, 1879." In *Marx and Engels Collected Works*, Vol. 45. Moscow: Progress Publishers, 1991.

——. "Marx to Edward Spencer Beesly, October 19, 1870." In *Marx and Engels Collected Works*, Vol. 44. Moscow: Progress Publishers, 1989.

——. "Marx to Ferdinand Domela Nieuwenhuis, February 22, 1881." In *Marx and Engels Collected Works*, Vol. 46. Moscow: Progress Publishers, 1992.

——. "Marx to Ferdinand Feckles, January 21, 1877." In *Marx and Engels Collected Works*, Vol. 45. Moscow: Progress Publishers, 1991.

——. "Marx to Ferdinand Freiligrath, February 29, 1860." In *Marx and Engels Collected Works*, Vol. 41. Moscow: Progress Publishers, 1985.

——. "Marx to Ferdinand Lassalle, January 16, 1861." In *Marx and Engels Collected Works*, Vol. 41. Moscow: Progress Publishers, 1985.

——. "Marx to Frederick Engels, February 11, 1851." In *Marx and Engels Collected Works*, Vol. 38. Moscow: Progress Publishers, 1982.

——. "Marx to Frederick Engels, December 19, 1860." In *Marx and Engels Collected Works*, Vol. 41. Moscow: Progress Publishers, 1985.

——. "Marx to Frederick Engels, June 18, 1862." In *Marx and Engels Collected Works*, Vol. 41. Moscow: Progress Publishers, 1985.

References

———. "Marx to Frederick Engels, February 13, 1863." In *Marx and Engels Collected Works*, Vol. 41. Moscow: Progress Publishers, 1985.

———. "Marx to Frederick Engels, November 4, 1864." In *Marx and Engels Collected Works*, Vol. 42. Moscow: Progress Publishers, 1987.

———. "Marx to Frederick Engels, February 18, 1865." In *Marx and Engels Collected Works*, Vol. 42. Moscow: Progress Publishers, 1987.

———. "Marx to Frederick Engels, September 26, 1868." In *Marx and Engels Collected Works*, Vol. 21. Moscow: Progress Publishers, 1985.

———. "Marx to Frederick Engels, September 29, 1868." In *Marx and Engels Collected Works*, Vol. 21. Moscow: Progress Publishers, 1985.

———. "Marx to Frederick Engels, October 10, 1868." In *Marx and Engels Collected Works*, Vol. 21. Moscow: Progress Publishers, 1985.

———. "Marx to Frederick Engels, September 6, 1870." In *Marx and Engels Collected Works*, Vol. 44. Moscow: Progress Publishers, 1989.

———. "Marx to Frederick Engels, September 10, 1879." In *Marx and Engels Collected Works*, Vol. 45. Moscow: Progress Publishers, 1991.

———. "Marx to Friedrich Adolph Sorge, June 14, 1876." In *Marx and Engels Collected Works*, Vol. 45. Moscow: Progress Publishers, 1991.

———. "Marx to Friedrich Adolph Sorge, October 19, 1877." In *Marx and Engels Collected Works*, Vol. 45. Moscow: Progress Publishers, 1991.

———. "Marx to Friedrich Adolph Sorge, September 19, 1879." In *Marx and Engels Collected Works*, Vol. 45. Moscow: Progress Publishers, 1991.

———. "Marx to Friedrich Adolph Sorge, November 5, 1880." In *Marx and Engels Collected Works*, Vol. 46. Moscow: Progress Publishers, 1992.

———. "Marx to Friedrich Bolte, November 23, 1871." In *Marx and Engels Collected Works*, Vol. 44. Moscow: Progress Publishers, 1989.

———. Marx to Johann Baptist von Schweitzer, October 13, 1868." In *Marx and Engels Collected Works*, Vol. 43. Moscow: Progress Publishers, 1988.

———. "Marx to Joseph Weydemeyer, March 5, 1852." In *Marx and Engels Collected Works*, Vol. 39. Moscow: Progress Publishers, 1983.

———. "Marx to Laura and Paul Lafargue, February 15, 1869." In *Marx and Engels Collected Works*, Vol. 43. Moscow: Progress Publishers, 1988.

References

———. "Marx to Ludwig Kugelmann, March 6, 1868." In *Marx and Engels Collected Works*, Vol. 42. Moscow: Progress Publishers, 1987.

———. "Marx to Ludwig Kugelmann, April 12, 1871." In *Marx and Engels Collected Works*, Vol. 44. Moscow: Progress Publishers, 1989.

———. "Marx to *Otechestvenniye Zapiski*, November 1877." In *Marx and Engels Collected Works*, Vol. 24. Moscow: Progress Publishers, 1989.

———. "Marx to Sigfrid Meyer, April 30, 1867." In *Marx and Engels Collected Works*, Vol. 42. Moscow: Progress Publishers, 1987.

———. "Marx to Vera Zasulich (First Draft), March 3, 1881." In *Marx and Engels Collected Works*, Vol. 42. Moscow: Progress Publishers, 1987.

———. "Marx to Vera Zasulich, March 8, 1881." In *Marx and Engels Collected Works*, Vol. 24. Moscow: Progress Publishers, 1989.

———. "Meeting of the Central Authority, September 15, 1850." In *Marx and Engels Collected Works*, Vol. 10. Moscow: Progress Publishers, 1978.

———. "Moralizing Criticism and Critical Morality: Contribution to German Cultural History Contra Karl Heinzen." In *Marx and Engels Collected Works*, Vol. 6. Moscow: Progress Publishers, 1976.

———. "Notes on Bakunin's Book *Statehood and Anarchy*." In *Marx and Engels Collected Works*, Vol. 24. Moscow: Progress Publishers, 1989.

———. "Notes on Wagner's *Lehrbuch der politischen Oekonomie*." In *Marx and Engels Collected Works*, Vol. 24. Moscow: Progress Publishers, 1989.

———. "On Proudhon." In *Marx and Engels Collected Works*, Vol. 20. Moscow: Progress Publishers, 1985.

———. "On the Hague Congress: A Correspondents Report of a Speech Made at a Meeting in Amsterdam on September 8, 1872." In *Marx and Engels Collected Works*, Vol. 23. Moscow: Progress Publishers, 1988.

———. "On the Jewish Question." In *Marx and Engels Collected Works*, Vol. 3. Moscow: Progress Publishers, 1975.

———. *Outlines of the Critique of Political Economy*. In *Marx and Engels Collected Works*, Vol. 28. Moscow: Progress Publishers, 1986.

———. *Outlines of the Critique of Political Economy*. In *Marx and Engels Collected Works*, Vol. 29. Moscow: Progress Publishers, 1987.

———. "Proceedings of the Sixth Rhine Province Assembly. First Article. Debates on Freedom of the Press and Publication of the

References

Proceedings of the Assembly of the Estates." In *Marx and Engels Collected Works*, Vol. 1. Moscow: Progress Publishers, 1975.

———. "Provisional Rules of the Association." In *Marx and Engels Collected Works*, Vol. 20. Moscow: Progress Publishers, 1985.

———. "Resolution of the General Council on Félix Pyatt's Provocative Behavior" *Marx and Engels Collected Works* 21. Moscow: Progress Publishers, 1985.

———. "Russian Policy Against Turkey and Chartism." In *Marx and Engels Collected Works*, Vol. 12. Moscow: Progress Publishers, 1979.

———. "Second Address of the General Council of the International Working Men's Association on the Franco-Prussian War." In *Marx and Engels Collected Works*, Vol. 22. Moscow: Progress Publishers, 1986.

———. "Second Draft of *The Civil War in France*." In *Marx and Engels Collected Works*, Vol. 22. Moscow: Progress Publishers, 1986.

———. "The Chartists." In *Marx and Engels Collected Works*, Vol. 11. Moscow: Progress Publishers, 1979.

———. *The Civil War in France*. In *Marx and Engels Collected Works*, Vol. 22. Moscow: Progress Publishers, 1986.

———. "The Communism of the *Rheinischer Beobachter*." In *Marx and Engels Collected Works*, Vol. 6. Moscow: Progress Publishers, 1976.

———. *The Eighteenth Brumaire of Louis Bonaparte*. In *Marx and Engels Collected Works*, Vol. 11. Moscow: Progress Publishers, 1979.

———. "The General Council to the Federal Council of Romance Switzerland." In *Marx and Engels Collected Works*, Vol. 21. Moscow: Progress Publishers, 1985.

———. *The Poverty of Philosophy*. In *Marx and Engels Collected Works*, Vol. 6. Moscow: Progress Publishers, 1976.

———. "The Value-Form," *Capital & Class* 2, no. 1 (1978): 131-33.

———. "Theses on Feuerbach." In *Marx and Engels Collected Works*, Vol. 5. Moscow: Progress Publishers, 1975.

———. "To the President and Executive Committee of the General Association of German Workers, August 18, 1868." In *Marx and Engels Collected Works*, Vol. 21. Moscow: Progress Publishers, 1985.

———. "Value, Price, and Profit." In *Marx and Engels Collected Works*, Vol. 20. Moscow: Progress Publishers, 1985.

———. "Wage Labor and Capital." In *Marx and Engels Collected Works*, Vol. 9. Moscow: Progress Publishers, 1977.

———. "Wages." In *Marx and Engels Collected Works*, Vol. 6. Moscow: Progress Publishers, 1976.

References

Marx, Karl and Frederick Engels, "Address of the Central Authority to the League, March 1850." In *Marx and Engels Collected Works*, Vol. 10. Moscow: Progress Publishers, 1978.

———. "Address of the German Democratic Communists of Brussels to Mr. Feargus O'Connor." In *Marx and Engels Collected Works*, Vol. 6. Moscow: Progress Publishers, 1976.

———. "Circular Letter, September 17-18, 1879." In *Marx and Engels Collected Works*, Vol. 45. Moscow: Progress Publishers, 1991.

———. "*Le socialisme et l'impôt, par Émile de Girardin.*" In *Marx and Engels Collected Works*, Vol. 10. Moscow: Progress Publishers, 1978.

———. "*Les Conspirateurs, par A. Chenu; ex-capitaine des gardes du citoyen Caussidière. Les societes secretes; la prefecture de police sous Caussidière; les corps-francs. La naissance de la Republique en fevrier 1848 par Lucien de la Hodde.*" In *Marx and Engels Collected Works*, Vol. 10. Moscow: Progress Publishers, 1978.

———. *Manifesto of the Communist Party.* In *Marx and Engels Collected Works*, Vol. 6. Moscow: Progress Publishers, 1976.

———. "Preface to the 1872 German Edition of the *Manifesto of the Communist Party.*" In *Marx and Engels Collected Works*, Vol. 23. Moscow: Progress Publishers, 1988.

———. "Resolutions of the Conference of Delegates of the International Working Men's Association." In *Marx and Engels Collected Works*, Vol. 22. Moscow: Progress Publishers, 1986.

———. "Resolutions of the General Congress Held at The Hague." In *Marx and Engels Collected Works*, Vol. 23. Moscow: Progress Publishers, 1988.

———. "Review, May to October (1850)." In *Marx and Engels Collected Works*, Vol. 10. Moscow: Progress Publishers, 1978.

———. *The German Ideology.* In *Marx and Engels Collected Works*, Vol. 5. Moscow: Progress Publishers, 1975.

———. *The Holy Family, or Critique of Critical Criticism.* In *Marx and Engels Collected Works*, Vol. 4. Moscow: Progress Publishers, 1975.

———. *Writings on the Paris Commune.* Edited by Hal Draper. New York: Monthly Review Press, 1971.

Maslow, Abraham H. *Motivation and Personality,* 2. ed. New York: Harper & Row, 1970.

McCarthy, George E. ed. *Marx and Aristotle: Nineteenth Century German Social Theory and Classical Antiquity.* Maryland: Rowman & Littlefield Publishers, Inc., 1992.

References

———. *Marx and Social Justice: Ethics and Natural Law in the Critique of Political Economy*. Leiden: Brill, 2017.

McLellan, David. *Karl Marx His Life and Thought*. (New York: Harper & Row, 1973.

Meisner, Maurice. *Marxism, Maoism, and Utopianism: Eight Essays*. Madison: The University of Wisconsin Press, 1982.

Merriman, John M. *Massacre: The Life and Death of the Paris Commune of 1871*. New Haven: Yale University Press, 2014.

Mészáros, István. *Marx's Theory of Alienation*. London: Merlin Press, 2005.

Moore, Stanley. *Marx on the Choice between Socialism and Communism*. Cambridge: Harvard University Press, 1980.

Moss, Bernard H. *The Origins of the French Labour Movement, 1830-1914: The Socialism of Skilled Workers*. Berkeley: University of California Press, 1976).

Most, Johann. *Kapital und Arbeit: Ein populärer Auszug aus "Das Kapital" von Karl Marx*, 2. edition. Chemnitz G. Rübner, 1876.

Musto, Marcello, ed. *Workers Unite! The International 150 Years Later*. New York: Bloomsbury, 2014.

Newman, Saul, ed. *Max Stirner*. Basingstoke: Palgrave Macmillan, 2011.

Nimtz, August H. Jr. *Marx and Engels: Their Contribution to Democratic Breakthrough* Albany: SUNY Press, 2000.

Nordahl, Richard. "Marx and Utopia: A Critique of the 'Orthodox' View." *Canadian Journal of Political Science / Revue canadienne de science politique* 20, no. 4 (1987): 755-83.

Obermann, Karl. *Joseph Weydemeyer: Pioneer of American Socialism*. New York: International Publishers, 1947.

Ollman, Bertell. *Alienation: Marx's Conception of Man in Capitalist Society*, 2. edition. London: Cambridge University Press, 1976.

Paden, Roger. "Marx's Critique of the Utopian Socialists." *Utopian Studies* 13, no. 2 (2002): 67-91.

Peffer, Rodney G. *Marxism, Morality, and Social Justice*. Princeton: Princeton University Press, 1990.

Plekhanov, Georgi. *Fundamental Problems of Marxism*. New York: International Publishers, 1969.

Popper, Karl. *The Open Society and Its Enemies: Hegel and Marx*, Volume 2, 7th edition. Princeton: Princeton University Press, 2006.

References

Riazanov, David. "The Relations of Marx with Blanqui." *Labor Monthly: A Magazine of International Labour* 10, no. 8 (1928): 492-97.

Rockmore, Tom. *Marx's Dream: From Capitalism to Communism.* Chicago: University of Chicago Press, 2018.

Rühle, Otto. *Karl Marx: His Life and Work.* Translated by Eden and Cedar Paul. Abingdon: Routledge, 2011 (1929).

Sayer, Derek. "The Critique of Politics and Political Economy: Capitalism, Communism, and the State in Marx's Writings of the Mid-1840s." *The Sociological Review* 33, no. 2 (1985): 221-53.

———. *The Violence of Abstraction: The Analytical Foundations of Historical Materialism.* Oxford: Basil Blackwell, 1987.

Sayers, Sean. *Marx and Alienation: Essays on Hegelian Themes.* Basingstoke: Palgrave Macmillan, 2011.

Schaff, Adam. *Marxism and the Human Individual.* New York: McGraw-Hill, 1970.

Schäffle, Albert. *The Quintessence of Socialism,* 8th edition. Translated by Bernard Bosanquet. London: Swan Sonnenschein & Co., 1891.

Schmidt, Alfred. *The Concept of Nature in Marx.* Translated by Ben Fowkes. London: Verso, 2014 (1962).

Schulkind, Eugene, ed. *The Paris Commune of 1871: The View From the Left.* New York: Grove Press, 1974.

Singh, Rustam. "Status of Violence in Marx's Theory of Revolution." *Economic and Political Weekly* 24, no. 4 (1989): 9-20.

Smith, Adam. *An Inquiry into the Nature and Causes of the Wealth of Nations.* Chicago: University of Chicago Press, 1976 (1776).

Tabak, Mehmet. *Dialectics of Human Nature in Marx's Philosophy.* New York: Palgrave, 2012.

———. *Hegel's Career and Politics: The Making of the Most Famous Philosopher in Germany, 1788-1831.* New York: Author, 2019.

Thomas, Paul. *Alien Politics: Marxist State Theory Retrieved.* New York: Routledge, 1994.

———. "Karl Marx and Max Stirner." *Political Theory* 3, no. 2 (1975): 159-79.

———. *Karl Marx and the Anarchists.* London: Routledge & Paul Kegan, 1980.

Tombs, Robert. *The Paris Commune of 1871.* London: Routledge, 1999.

References

Tucker, Robert C. *Philosophy and Myth in Karl Marx*. Cambridge: Cambridge University Press, 1961.

Wada, Haruki. "Marx and Revolutionary Russia." In *Late Marx And the Russian Road: Marx and "the Peripheries of Capitalism,"* edited by Teodor Shanin. New York: Monthly Review Press, 1983.

Wallimann, Isidor. *Estrangement: Marx's Conception of Human Nature and the Division of Labor*. Westport: Greenwood Press, 1981.

Ware, Robert. "Marx, the Division of Labor, and Human Nature." *Social Theory and Practice* 8, no. 1 (1982): 43-71.

Webb, Darren. *Marx, Marxism, and Utopia*. Burlington: Ashgate, 2000.

Wilde, Lawrence. *Ethical Marxism and its Radical Critics*. Basingstoke: MacMillan Press, 1998.

Wood, Allen W. *Karl Marx*, 2. ed. New York: Routledge, 2004.

———. "The Marxian Critique of Justice." *Philosophy & Public Affairs* 1, no. 3 (1972): 244-82.

Wood, Ellen M. "Historical Materialism in 'Forms which Precede Capitalist Production'." In *Karl Marx's Grundrisse: Foundations of the Critique of Political Economy 150 Years Later*, edited by Marcello Musto. London: Routledge, 2008.